DISASTERS

DISAS

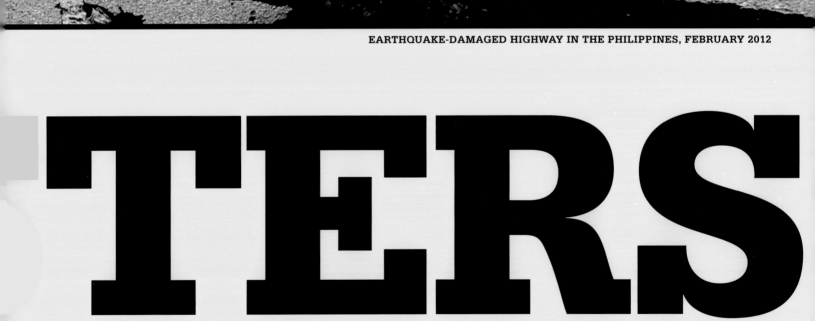

EARTHQUAKE-DAMAGED HIGHWAY IN THE PHILIPPINES, FEBRUARY 2012

TERS

DAVID BURNIE

SCHOLASTIC discover more™

Storm Chasers digital book

Your free digital companion book, Storm Chasers, is packed with more information and images about the heroic men and women who study disasters and try to prevent them, every day of their working lives.

Your digital book is very simple to use. Enter the code (bottom right) to download it to any Mac or PC. Open it in Adobe Reader, also free to download. Then you're all set!

Hurricane Hunters

Each year between June and November, the men and women of the 53rd Weather **Reconnaissance** Squadron (WRS) – part of the US Air Force Reserve – risk their lives and fly directly into the hearts of hurricanes. Known as the Hurricane Hunters, they gather as much data as they can on these vast, wild tropical storms, which can devastate coastal regions. The information that the Hurricane Hunters collect in their Lockheed Martin C-130J aircraft helps meteorologists make more accurate forecasts, so people can be evacuated from the paths of storms and lives can be saved.

See a pow

Shirley M

100 million:
the approximate number of US citizens at risk from hurricane strikes

STORM CI
and Other Disaster He
A digital companion to Disasters

Storm warnings
If weather satellites detect a tropical storm, the **National Hurricane Center** in Miami, Florida, contacts the 53rd WRS so that aircraft can be sent up to investigate.

Robots in the sky
NASA, the US space agency, uses unpiloted **drone** aircraft to study the formation and intensity of hurricanes. Drones can stay airborne for twice as long as a C-130J plane.

Flying laboratory
The C-130J is a military transport plane adapted for weather research. Packed with scientific instruments, it has four powerful turboprop engines that can keep it flying for up to 14 hours as it tracks hurricanes.

 **discover more**—the 53rd WRS

Hyperlinks
All of the pages in the digital book are hyperlinked. Click the coloured buttons for more facts and pictures, video clips, personal accounts, and tips for using your digital book.

Disaster heroes
In Storm Chasers, you'll meet scientists who risk their lives by rushing right into a hurricane, a tornado, or a volcano spewing lava, and rescuers who refuse to give up, even in the most terrifying circumstances.

"Flying into a hurricane, . . . you feel like you're on a rollercoaster – for 10 hours!"
—SHIRLEY MURILLO, RESEARCH METEOROLOGIST

High fliers [53rd Weather Reconnaissance Squadron]

Weather satellites can spot tropical storms forming and track their movements, but they cannot measure conditions deep inside a hurricane. That's where the 53rd WRS comes in. The extra information gathered by its crews is crucial for determining the intensity of the hurricane and how it may develop.

The most dangerous part of any hurricane-hunting mission is flying through the doughnut-shaped band of thunderstorms surrounding the eye, or calm centre, of the hurricane. This band, known as the eye wall, is the most violent part of the hurricane, and it is the region that causes most damage if the hurricane moves inland. Here, the WRS's plane may be lashed by driving rain and hail, buffeted by winds that can exceed 240 kph (155 mph), and tossed by violent updrafts and downdrafts. The 53rd's C-130J aircraft usually flies an X-shaped path through the hurricane, passing right though it once then turning and crossing it again at an angle to the first fly-through. Weather experts analyse the data collected by the plane's own sensors, by dropsondes launched into the hurricane, and by floating buoys dropped into the sea ahead of the storm. The National Hurricane Center (NHC) can then issue warnings if it looks as if the hurricane may strike land.

A pilot and co-pilot fly a C-130J.

This is the uniform badge of the 53rd WRS, based in Biloxi, MS. The Hurricane Hunters have been flying right into the heart of storms since 1944.

"It's an awesome job to not only be inside Mother Nature, but to help so many people."
—Captain Nicole Mitchell, 53rd WRS, US Air Force Reserve

Hunting the hurricane

Weather officers study the data before sending it to the NHC.

Alerted by the NHC, a C-130J prepares to taxi out for takeoff.

Radar helps the navigator guide the plane to the hurricane.

The loadmaster releases a buoy which falls into the sea below.

The plane enters the eye.

A dropsonde is loaded into a chute for launching into the hurricane.

Supercell

A supercell is an intense, long-lasting thunderstorm that contains a continuously rotating updraft of air. Supercells typically have a lifespan of about three hours, but some rage for as long as six. They cause severe weather, including huge hailstones, torrential rain, and strong winds—and sometimes even tornadoes.

Supercells usually occur when warm, humid, low-pressure air is below a cooler upper layer. As the warmer air rises and the cooler air descends, the interaction between the warm updrafts and cool downdrafts generates a spinning column of warm air.

Large supercells sometimes generate tornadoes, especially during warmer times of the year. The base of a supercell has a low, rotating bulge known as a wall cloud, which hangs beneath the broader cloud layer above. It is from the wall cloud that tornadoes may develop.

Only about 30 percent of supercells produce tornadoes, and not all tornadoes are formed by supercells. However, when they do occur, supercell tornadoes are often extremely violent—with winds that can exceed 320 kph (200 mph)—and they may stay in contact with the ground for an hour or more. A single supercell thunderstorm can generate several tornadoes.

21,000 m:
(70,000 feet)
the height of the clouds in the tallest supercell thunderstorms

In-depth info

To discover even more, click the coloured words to link to encyclopedia pages with in-depth articles on essential topics. Glossary entries explain difficult terms.

Project Editor: Sue Nicholson
Project Art Editors: Emma Forge, Tom Forge
Art Director: Bryn Walls
Managing Editor: Miranda Smith
Managing Production Editor: Stephanie Engel
Illustrator: Tim Loughhead, Precision Illustration
Cover Designer: Neal Cobourne
DTP: Sunita Gahir, John Goldsmid
Visual Content Project Manager:
Diane Allford-Trotman
Executive Director of Photography, Scholastic:
Steve Diamond

"I am never afraid, because I have seen so many eruptions in 23 years that even if I die tomorrow, I don't care"

—FRENCH VOLCANOLOGIST MAURICE KRAFFT,
THE DAY BEFORE HE DIED IN AN ERUPTION OF
MOUNT UNZEN, JAPAN, 1991

Library of Congress Cataloging-in-Publication Data Available
Distributed in the UK by Scholastic UK Ltd, Westfield Road, Southam, Warwickshire, England CV47 0RA

ISBN 978-1-407-13653-0

10 9 8 7 6 5 4 3 2 1   13 14 15 16 17

Printed in Singapore   46
First published 2013

Scholastic is constantly working to lessen the environmental impact of our manufacturing processes. To view our industry-leading paper procurement policy, visit www.scholastic.com/paperpolicy.

CAR SUBMERGED IN VOLCANIC ASH, CHAITÉN, CHILE, 2009

Contents

Haiti in ruins

Disaster struck the Caribbean country of Haiti on 12 January 2010, when a massive earthquake devastated the country's capital, Port-au-Prince. In less than a minute, over a quarter of a million homes collapsed, often with people trapped inside. As many as 316,000 people may have died, and city streets remained blocked with rubble for months (see pages 50–51).

Dangerously close

Photographer Mitchell Krog risked his life to take this image of three enormous bolts of lightning striking the ground around the Voortrekker Monument in Pretoria, South Africa. This country experiences many lightning storms. In 2011, lightning killed 15 people within a single weekend.

Disas
wea

* How do tornadoes form?

* What is the most deadly type of lightning?

* Which hurricane devastated a whole city?

trous

ther

A deadly year

A natural disaster strikes almost every month somewhere around the world. In 2010, disasters included tornadoes, wildfires, floods, and a catastrophic earthquake in Haiti.

Around the world

No place is completely safe from natural disasters. Volcanic eruptions and earthquakes occur at fault lines on Earth's surface, while extreme weather can cause disasters all over the globe. Some weather-related disasters, such as tornadoes, cause havoc within minutes. Others, such as droughts, start slowly and take months or even years to unfold.

BLIZZARD: NORTH AMERICA, FEBRUARY – 10+ KILLED

TORNADO OUTBREAK: US MIDWEST, JUNE – 12 KILLED

TORRENTIAL RAIN: MEXICO, FEBRUARY – 28 KILLED

Hurricane Alex
Alex hit Mexico and the United States in June, killing at least 12 people.

NORTH AMERICA

US

MEXICO

Haiti earthquake
An earthquake struck without warning on 12 January.

EUROPE

HAITI

NIGER

SOUTH AMERICA

Chile earthquake
A magnitude 8.8 earthquake struck in February, leaving more than 500 dead.

CHILE

Drought: Niger and other countries in the Sahel region of Africa

10 million hungry

Earthquake: Haiti

Haiti, one of the world's poorest nations, was unprepared when it was struck by a colossal earthquake. Many buildings collapsed, leaving around 1 million people homeless.

Haiti

Caribbean Sea

SOUTH AMERICA

316,000 killed

(official estimate from the Haitian government)

An estimated

400,000

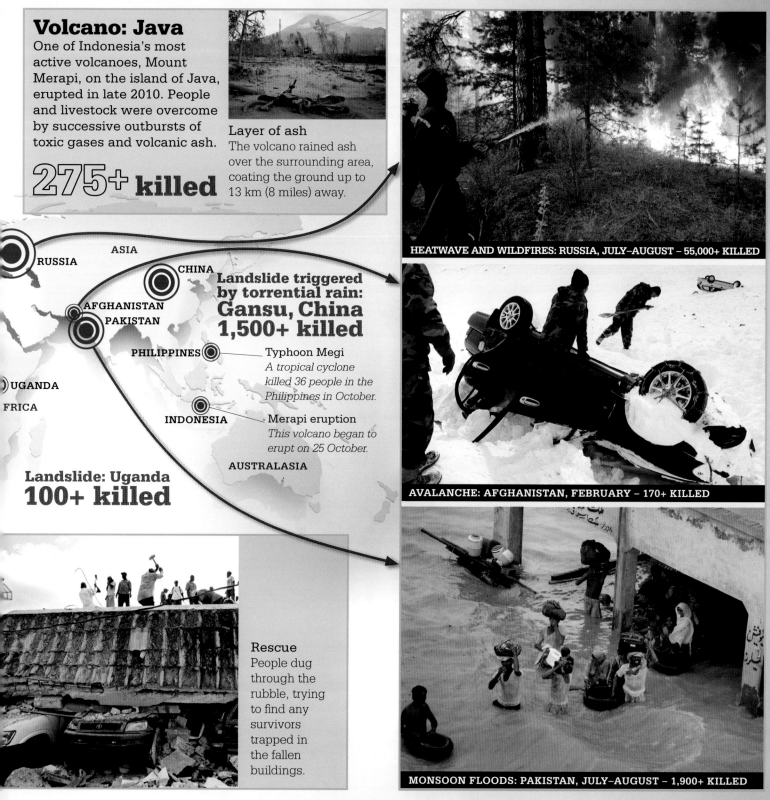

Volcano: Java

One of Indonesia's most active volcanoes, Mount Merapi, on the island of Java, erupted in late 2010. People and livestock were overcome by successive outbursts of toxic gases and volcanic ash.

275+ killed

Layer of ash
The volcano rained ash over the surrounding area, coating the ground up to 13 km (8 miles) away.

HEATWAVE AND WILDFIRES: RUSSIA, JULY–AUGUST – 55,000+ KILLED

Landslide triggered by torrential rain:
Gansu, China 1,500+ killed

Typhoon Megi
A tropical cyclone killed 36 people in the Philippines in October.

Merapi eruption
This volcano began to erupt on 25 October.

Landslide: Uganda
100+ killed

AVALANCHE: AFGHANISTAN, FEBRUARY – 170+ KILLED

Rescue
People dug through the rubble, trying to find any survivors trapped in the fallen buildings.

MONSOON FLOODS: PAKISTAN, JULY–AUGUST – 1,900+ KILLED

people died in natural disasters in 2010 (excluding famine)

ASIA • RUSSIA • CHINA • AFGHANISTAN • PAKISTAN • PHILIPPINES • UGANDA • AFRICA • INDONESIA • AUSTRALASIA

Weather machine

Weather is the state of the atmosphere anywhere above Earth. In some places, it stays calm and settled for months. In others, it switches between calm and stormy, with dangerous extremes of rain, drought, heat, and cold.

Restless air

This satellite image of Earth shows swirling clouds moving through the atmosphere. Clouds are a visible part of our planet's weather machine – a complex cycle of air and water set in motion by the Sun.

Sun power
The Sun's energy warms land, water, and air at different rates. Clouds form when warmed air rises. As it cools, it condenses into billions of tiny water droplets or ice crystals, which float in the air.

Polar jet stream
This narrow band of cold, fast-moving air can trigger extreme weather, such as snowstorms and floods, when it shifts.

Heat energy from the Sun

Atmosphere

Scientists divide the atmosphere into five layers. Each layer gets less dense, or thinner, the farther you travel from Earth's surface, because there is less air pressing down from above.

Exosphere: 600–10,000 km (375–6,200 miles)
Satellites orbit Earth in this layer. From here, the air's gas molecules and atoms escape into space.

Thermosphere: 90–600 km (56–375 miles)
Lights called auroras flicker in this layer of the upper atmosphere.

Mesosphere: 50–90 km (31–56 miles)
Meteors burn up in this layer, leaving fiery trails in the sky.

Stratosphere: 20–50 km (12–31 miles)
This layer contains some high-level, icy clouds.

Troposphere: 0–20 km (0–12 miles)
This is the layer we live in, where our weather occurs.

The weather layer
Weather happens in the troposphere, the layer of air just above Earth's surface. This layer contains nearly all of the atmosphere's water, and most of its clouds.

Doldrums
This band of hot, humid air stretching around the Equator is the site of frequent thunderstorms.

85 km (50 miles) the height of the world's highest clouds

Mid-latitude storm

Weather front

Cloudy skies

Different clouds form depending on the altitude warm air rises to, and its temperature. Streams of converging air, forced to rise when they meet, cause cumulus clouds and showers. Strong, rapidly cooling updrafts can create thunderclouds.

Mid-latitude storm damage

Mid-latitude storms start where a mass of cold polar air meets warmer air from the middle latitudes north and south of the Equator, forming storm clouds. This type of storm occurs in both the Northern and Southern Hemispheres.

Thunderstorm

Floods and landslides may occur when thunderstorms bring torrential rain. These local storms form when warm, moist air rises rapidly over land or sea, building into huge, towering thunderclouds.

Hurricane Dean, 2007

Huge storms like Hurricane Dean are generated by heat stored in the oceans, which rises to form moisture-filled clouds. Strong winds set the clouds spinning, often forming giant spirals (see pages 26–27).

Weather front

Long rows of clouds show where different air masses meet. This meeting-place is called a weather front. Weather fronts often result in changeable weather, such as rain or snow, across a whole region.

Weather scientists [At work]

Our world is warming, and weather patterns are changing. This climate rollercoaster is causing more thunderstorms, floods, hurricanes, droughts, tornadoes, and wildfires. Meteorologists (weather scientists) monitor the changes and warn us about extreme weather events that could be heading our way. It is exciting and sometimes dangerous work.

Into the clouds

Meteorologists work hard to predict severe weather accurately. They collect evidence from ground stations all around the world. They use satellites to observe the movements of storms. Some scientists risk their lives and chase the storms themselves, launching weather balloons that carry equipment directly into thunderclouds. The balloons take atmospheric measurements, such as air pressure, which help scientists predict the movement of weather fronts.

Storm study

Scientists from the Severe Thunderstorm Electrification and Precipitation Study (STEPS) prepare to launch electric-field meters and a radiosonde into a thunderstorm on the plains of Colorado. Their goal is to learn how a storm produces electricity and lightning. Giant storms like these are dangerous because they can generate tornadoes.

Eyewitness

NAME: Don MacGorman

DATE: 22 June 2000

LOCATION: Northeast Colorado

DETAILS: Don MacGorman was one of the leaders of the STEPS mobile weather ballooning team, investigating the lightning within storm clouds.

" I remember the tension and excitement I felt as we hunted a storm and manoeuvered into position to launch this balloon. Seeing the balloon rise smoothly toward the storm was quite a thrill. But then hail started falling, so we had to rush to our vehicles to avoid getting hurt. "

Weather tech

Scientists can measure air movements in supercell thunderclouds and "see" tornadoes as they form. They use Doppler radar to measure the speed of water droplets as they swirl in tornadoes or thunderclouds. The radar sends out a microwave beam that bounces off the droplets. The returning echoes have varying pitches, which can be used to create an image of the storm.

Doppler on wheels
A mobile Doppler radar truck scans a severe thunderstorm in the Texas panhandle – a region often hit by tornadoes.

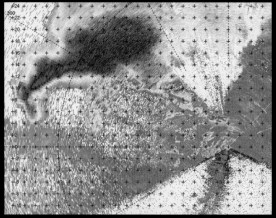

Birth of a tornado
This Doppler radar image shows the typical hook-shaped echo (in red) of a tornado, forming on the edge of a supercell thunderstorm.

Field to forecast

To predict extreme weather, meteorologists need to know what the weather is doing now. This information comes from many sources, including automatic weather stations and geostationary satellites. Once the data has been gathered, it is fed into supercomputers, which forecast the weather several days ahead. Extreme weather triggers an automatic alert that is broadcast to warn people.

1 Data gathering
A geostationary satellite above the Atlantic Ocean is used to track a hurricane. To see temperature contrasts, the satellite takes images in both infrared and visible light.

2 Data processing
The satellite data is processed by supercomputers. These create atmospheric models, which simulate the ways the hurricane may develop over the next few days.

3 Emergency alerts
Weather models are used to produce regional forecasts and weather warnings. If the hurricane approaches land, warnings give people enough time to leave the area.

Work of climatologists

Climatologists study Earth's long-term weather patterns. They use data from weather records combined with other kinds of evidence, such as ice cores (long cylinders of ice taken from ice sheets), to study past climates. The research shows that the world is warming at a dangerous rate (see pages 86–89), and that humans are probably to blame.

Ice core sampling
Scientists in Greenland extract an ice core sample. Ice cores contain bubbles of ancient air, showing what the climate was like thousands of years ago.

Air bubbles in ice cores tell scientists that **CO_2 levels are at their highest in 440,000 years**

Tornadoes [Killer twisters]

Reaching down from stormy skies, tornadoes are short-lived but unleash some of the fastest winds on Earth, often leaving a trail of devastation.

Life of a tornado

Tornadoes are formed beneath supercells, or rotating thunderstorms, when a funnel drops from a cloud and makes contact with the ground. Most tornadoes last 10–15 minutes. Rare, powerful ones may last for about an hour.

Inside a tornado

A tornado contains a low-pressure core, surrounded by a condensation funnel. Air rushes in and spirals around the funnel, while a powerful downdraft sucks air through the funnel towards the ground.

Danger zone

Extreme tornadoes can have wind speeds of up to 500 kph (310 mph) and be around 76 m (240 feet) wide.

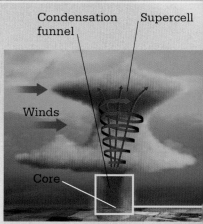

Condensation funnel   Supercell

Winds

Core

SUPERCELL

1 Funnel forming
A funnel of air reaches down from a cloud at the base of a rotating supercell. The funnel gains speed as it spins.

2 Touching the ground
The funnel lengthens until it reaches the ground. Dust and debris stirred up by the wind form a sleeve around the core.

3 Maturing
Whirling winds at the base scour the ground. The tornado is now at its maximum strength.

Around 1,000 tornadoes

Tornado aftermath

The town of Joplin, Missouri, lies in ruins after an EF5 tornado (see page 24) swept across it, leaving a path of destruction 1.6 km (1 mile) wide and killing 158 people.

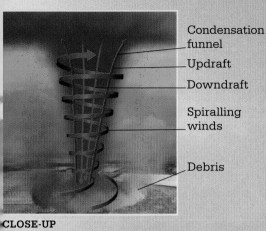

Condensation funnel
Updraft
Downdraft
Spiralling winds
Debris

CLOSE-UP

Danger signs

Tornadoes can develop within minutes, so it is important to be aware of the danger signs. The first warning for people in an area prone to tornadoes usually comes from the TV or radio. On average, people have only 10–15 minutes to find shelter after hearing a warning.

Tornado warning signs:
- Dark, often greenish sky
- Large hail
- A massive, dark, low-lying cloud (particularly if rotating)
- A loud roar, similar to a freight train's

STORM SHELTER ↑

Shelter Underground shelters provide some protection from winds and flying debris.

Giant hailstones Hailstones the size of tennis balls, each weighing up to 1 kg (2.2 lbs), can be an extra hazard during some storms.

4 Shrinking and slowing
Although still powerful, the tornado's wind speeds start to drop. As the tornado weakens, it starts to tilt and lose its shape.

5 Fading away
The tilt increases, heavy debris drops to the ground, and the tornado fades away. Rare, powerful ones may last about an hour.

hit the USA every year

Eyewitness

NAME: Dr Kevin Kikta

DATE: 22 May 2011

LOCATION: Joplin, Missouri, USA

DETAILS: Dr Kikta was one of two emergency room doctors on duty at St John's Regional Medical Centre in Joplin on the day the tornado struck.

❝ We heard a loud horrifying sound like a large locomotive ripping through the hospital. . . . We heard glass shattering, . . . walls collapsing, people screaming, the ceiling caving in above us. . . . The whole process took about 45 seconds, but seemed like eternity. ❞

"**Driving into the heart of a tornado** was both exhilarating and scary. Inside that howling, sand-blasting wind, the **whole vehicle was shaking.** After the initial impact, once I knew we would be all right, I was able to relax enough to enjoy the moment. **"** —Sean Casey, 2009

Storm chasers

In 2009 and 2010, "storm chaser" Sean Casey crisscrossed the American Midwest in the ultimate tornado-proof machine. Called the Tornado Intercept Vehicle (TIV-2), it filmed a team of over 100 scientists involved in the VORTEX2 project – a mission to discover how and why tornadoes form. By collecting more information about these deadly storms, scientists hope to increase warning times and therefore save lives.

On 5 June 2009, the VORTEX2 team made history when they intercepted a tornado and filmed its entire life cycle.

11:30 AM	The team drove to Wyoming, where supercell storms were forecast for that day.
2:00 PM	They headed to a supercell located in Goshen County.
3:00 PM	The team set up Doppler radar equipment to scan the storm.
3:37 PM	A tornado warning was issued.
4:07 PM	The tornado touched down near La Grange, Wyoming.
4:10 PM	The team experienced softball-size hail.
4:31 PM	The tornado faded away, and the warning was lifted.

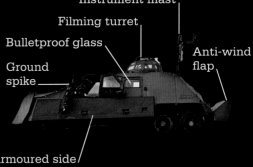

Instrument mast

Filming turret

Bulletproof glass

Anti-wind flap

Ground spike

Armoured side panel

Tornado Intercept Vehicle (TIV-2)
The 7-tonne TIV-2 has drop-down panels to prevent strong winds from blowing underneath it, and hydraulic spikes that anchor it to the ground.

Tornado facts and stats

Tornadoes strike in every continent except Antarctica. The United States tops the danger list, followed by Canada and Bangladesh. Tornadoes often hit cities and towns, and they can be more deadly than lightning. Oklahoma City, in the heart of Tornado Alley, has been hit by over 140 tornadoes since 1890. In 1974, it was struck by 5 twisters in a single day.

Tornado scale

The Enhanced Fujita (EF) scale rates tornado strength based on estimated wind speed and damage caused. EF0 tornadoes damage signs and break off small branches. EF5 tornadoes can flatten buildings.

Wind speeds and damage

EF0: 105–137 kph (65–85 mph)	Minor damage
EF1: 138–178 kph (86–110 mph)	Moderate damage
EF2: 179–218 kph (111–135 mph)	Considerable damage
EF3: 219–266 kph (136–165 mph)	Severe damage
EF4: 267–322 kph (166–200 mph)	Devastating damage
EF5: 322+ kph (200+ mph)	Total devastation

Blown away

People have reported seeing all sorts of things being picked up and carried by twisters. These range from lightweight paper to animals, cars, and trailers.

PEOPLE

COWS

FREIGHT TRAINS

DOGS

SCHOOL BUSES

FISH

MATTRESSES

CARS

Whirling record

Teenager Matt Suter holds the record for the longest distance a person has been blown along by a tornado. He was carried 398 m (1,307 feet) – and he survived!

Pressure drop

Air pressure inside a tornado's funnel can be 10 percent lower than the air pressure outside. Low pressure and powerful winds allow tornadoes to shift heavy objects, such as cars.

Tornadoes have an average height of

100–300 metres
(328–980 ft)
depending upon climate conditions

Bank cheque stubs broke the record for the **longest** measured flight of tornado debris:

359 km
(223 miles)

Tornado Alley

The midwestern states are famous for tornadoes, with 300 to 400 striking every year. Nicknamed "Tornado Alley", this region consists of flat, open plains where cold and warm air fronts often meet, creating the perfect mix for violent supercell thunderstorms. Tornadoes are also common in the Gulf Coast states, including Alabama and Florida.

Tornadoes per year 1953–2004

Between 1953 and 2004, Texas had more tornadoes than any other state, with an average of 139 a year.

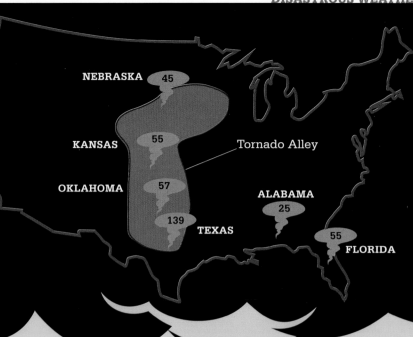

NEBRASKA 45
KANSAS 55
OKLAHOMA 57
TEXAS 139
Tornado Alley
ALABAMA 25
FLORIDA 55

Veering off

Tornadoes are usually steered by storms. In Tornado Alley, they often move from southwest to northeast.

511 kph: (318 mph)
the fastest wind speed measured in a tornado

The fastest recorded ground speed:
117 kph (78 mph)
reached by the 1925 Tri-State Tornado

Travelling at an average speed of
50 kph (31 mph)
a tornado can outpace an Olympic sprinter

Peak times

In the United States, tornadoes occur throughout the year, but they are most common on warm afternoons in spring and early summer.

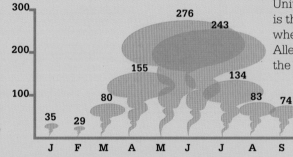

300
200
100

35 29 80 155 276 243 134 83 74 61 58 24
J F M A M J J A S O N D

Month by month

From 1991 to 2010, May and June were the top two months for tornadoes in the United States. This is the time of year when the Tornado Alley states have the most twisters.

Hit and miss

Although large tornadoes can kill hundreds of people, every year there are lucky escapes. In April 2012, a swarm of tornadoes struck Texas, but not one person died. The tornadoes hit during the day, and many people were able to reach shelter in time.

Tragic figures

Bangladesh holds the record for the most deaths in a single tornado strike.

695:
the number of people killed in the Tri-State Tornado outbreak in 1925, which struck Missouri, Illinois, and Indiana

1,300:
the number of people killed in Bangladesh by a single tornado in 1989

How a hurricane works

Hurricanes and typhoons are tropical cyclones: the world's most violent storms. Most form in late summer over warm, sun-drenched seas. Their winds can gust over 252 kph (157 mph), causing colossal damage if they drift over land.

How hurricanes form

Hurricanes form when the ocean's temperature is at least 27°C (80.5°F). Surface winds suck up moisture from the sea, creating rows of thunderclouds.

Eye wall
This inner ring of thunderstorms can drop 25 cm (10 ins) of rain in a single hour.

Spreading out
Cool, dry air flows outwards from the centre, sucking up more air from below.

Eye of the storm
The eye is a calm, warm area at the storm's centre.

Spiralling winds
Powerful winds spiral around the eye, sucking up water vapour from the sea.

Low pressure
Air pressure in the eye is lower than elsewhere in the storm.

Suction effect
Low air pressure in the eye raises the sea level below, creating a storm surge if the hurricane drifts over land.

Wind direction
Winds blow anti-clockwise in the Northern Hemisphere and clockwise in the Southern Hemisphere.

Force of the wind
A 4x4 lies crushed beneath a truck blown over in strong winds, as Hurricane Jeanne hits Florida in September 2004.

Life of a hurricane

These satellite images show Hurricane Katrina, which battered New Orleans in 2005 (see pages 28–29). The pictures are colour-coded to indicate the sea's surface temperature: red and orange are warmest, while blue is cold.

1 **Tropical depression and storm**
A tropical depression over the sea grew into a tropical storm, with wind speeds of more than 63 kph (39 mph).

2 **Category 1 hurricane**
The storm became a Category 1 hurricane when its winds gusted to over 119 kph (74 mph).

3 **Category 3 hurricane**
The hurricane intensified to Category 3, fuelled as it sucked up moisture crossing the Gulf of Mexico.

Cross-section]

Reaching the top
The top of a tropical cyclone can tower 15 km (8 miles) above the sea's surface.

Giant stretch
The biggest tropical cyclones are up to 800 km (500 miles) in diameter.

An inside view
If you could slice through a hurricane, you would see walls of clouds spiralling around its calm central eye. The spiral is made up of giant bands of rain. It rotates because Earth rotates.

Rain bands
Warm, moist air rises and creates bands of thunderclouds, separated by zones of clearer air.

Measuring hurricanes
Hurricane strength is measured on the Saffir-Simpson scale. Category 1 hurricanes cause little damage. Category 5 storms can tear off roofs and flood buildings far inland.

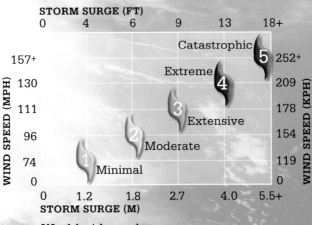

STORM SURGE (FT)
0   4   6   9   13   18+

WIND SPEED (MPH)
157+
130
111
96
74
0

Catastrophic 5 252+
Extreme 4 209
3 178
Extensive
2 154
Moderate
1 119
Minimal 0

WIND SPEED (KPH)

STORM SURGE (M)
0   1.2   1.8   2.7   4.0   5.5+

Worldwide scale
The Saffir-Simpson scale measures the strengths of all tropical cyclones, including hurricanes and typhoons.

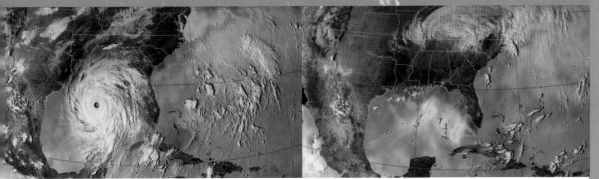

9 days:
the lifetime of a typical hurricane

4 Maximum-strength hurricane
Katrina briefly became a Category 5 hurricane as it drifted over land. Here, the eye is clearly visible at the centre of the spiral.

5 Tropical storm and depression
The hurricane weakened into a tropical storm, then into a depression, as it tracked northwards across the United States.

More here
For key to symbols, see page 112

air pressure cyclone eye wall **landfall** **tropical storm** tropics

Hurricane
by Terry Trueman

Riding Out the Hurricane
by Maeve McMahon

Check government information about what to do before, during, and after an emergency if you live in or are visiting an area prone to tropical cyclones.

Follow real-time warnings of tropical cyclones at:
http://www.nhc.noaa.gov
http://www.weather.gov.hk
http://www.bom.gov.au/cyclone

storm surge: a rise in sea level caused when a hurricane or typhoon drifts over land.

tropical cyclone: a powerful tropical storm that often forms over the sea.

tropical depression: a low-pressure weather system with heavy rain and clouds.

tropical storm: a storm that starts in the tropics – warm regions that lie north and south of the Equator.

Hurricane Katrina [Timeline]

In 2005, Hurricane Katrina struck the Gulf Coast of the United States. The storm caused chaos in New Orleans as floodwaters surged through the streets, killing more than 1,800 people and making thousands homeless.

25 AUG. (6:30 PM)
Florida
The hurricane struck the tip of Florida. Wind speeds reached 130 kph (80 mph); 14 people were killed and around 1 million lost power to their homes.

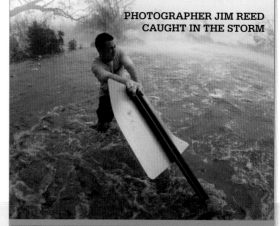

PHOTOGRAPHER JIM REED CAUGHT IN THE STORM

23 AUG.
Tropical depression
The National Hurricane Center in Florida issued a weather warning about a tropical depression forming over the Bahamas.

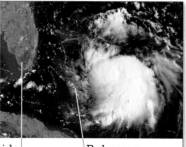

TROPICAL DEPRESSION TRACKING WEST

Florida | Bahamas

24 AUG.
The tropical depression strengthened into a storm and was named Tropical Storm Katrina – the 11th named storm of 2005.

26 AUG.
The National Hurricane Center predicted that Katrina would head east towards the Gulf Coast. The governor of Louisiana declared a state of emergency.

28 AUG. (7 AM)
Katrina strengthened into a Category 5 hurricane, with wind speeds of up to 280 kph (175 mph).

23/8 · 25/8 · 27/8 · 28/8

26 AUG.
Hurricane Katrina weakened into a tropical storm, but started to grow again as it moved across the warm waters of the Gulf of Mexico.

27 AUG.
Katrina became a Category 3 hurricane. Authorities advised people to leave New Orleans. Roads were jammed as people fled the city.

28 AUG. (5 PM)
The National Weather Service described Katrina as "potentially catastrophic".

25 AUG. (5 PM)
Hurricane
Tropical Storm Katrina became a Category 1 hurricane, with wind speeds of 119–153 kph (74–95 mph).

SATELLITE IMAGE OF KATRINA

28 AUG.
Press conference
At a morning press conference, after Katrina was upgraded to a Category 5 hurricane, the mayor of New Orleans, Ray Nagin, ordered residents to evacuate the city.

MAYOR RAY NAGIN

New Orleans mayor Ray Nagin:
"We are facing a storm that most of us have long feared"

28 AUG.
Taking shelter
Those who had not been able to leave New Orleans took shelter in the Louisiana Superdome.

LINING UP OUTSIDE THE SUPERDOME

1 SEPT.
Chaos in the city
New Orleans was in turmoil, with people raiding stores for food, medicine, and clean drinking water. The US government sent in troops to tackle the widespread crime.

FLOODED CITY STREETS

1.5 million evacuated
from Louisiana

4 SEPT.
Rescue

SAVING THE STRANDED

Thousands of people were taken to safety, and law and order was finally restored in the city.

30 AUG.
Katrina weakened into a tropical storm and caused heavy rainfall in the state of Tennessee.

31 AUG.
Katrina became a tropical depression. Its remnants caused heavy rain in Canada.

29/8 • 31/8 • 1/9 2/9 • 4/9 2006

31 AUG.
In New Orleans, around 100,000 people were still stranded, and 25,000 were in the Superdome. Water levels stopped rising.

2 SEPT.
Troops and supply trucks distributed food, clean drinking water, blankets, and first-aid kits.

5 SEPT.
Floodwaters receded. However, most of New Orleans lay empty and in ruins.

Aftermath
The process of rebuilding the city of New Orleans began.

29 AUG. (10 AM)
New Orleans
Winds of up to 160 kph (100 mph) and heavy rain struck New Orleans. Levees (artificial banks that prevent flooding) failed. Water started pouring through the streets until 80 percent of the city was underwater, in some places up to 6 m (20 feet) deep.

SATELLITE VIEW OF FLOODING

2006
Survivor stories

DRAWINGS BY DENISHA

Children who lived through Katrina told of their experiences through stories and art. These pictures by Denisha show her house before and after the storm.

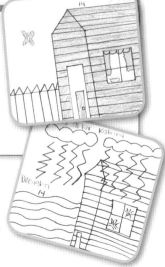

"**Before** the storm, there was always something good to eat on our stove"
—Denisha, Katrina's Kids Project

Seeking shelter

Battered by 145-kph (90-mph) winds, Key West residents struggle against Hurricane Georges as it smashes its way through southern Florida, USA. The hurricane, which formed off the African coast in September 1998, killed about 600 people in the Caribbean before striking the USA.

When lightning strikes

Awesome and exciting, lightning is perhaps the most spectacular show on Earth. Yet it can also be deadly. Every year, lightning strikes approximately 100,000 people around the world, killing 20,000 of them.

Global lightning

As you read this, there are about 2,000 thunderstorms taking place somewhere around the world. Warm regions get the most lightning – central Africa tops the list, followed by other places on or near the Equator.

Hot spots
This image shows the concentration of lightning storms around the globe.

Lightning types

There are different kinds of lightning, and some occur during the same storm. Heat from a lightning bolt sends shockwaves through the air, creating the crash or rumble of thunder.

Cloud to ground
This is the most common and deadly type of lightning. A bolt starts from a cloud, strikes the ground, then flashes back up the same path.

Cloud to cloud
In many thunderstorms, lightning flashes between clouds without touching the ground. If the bolt is obscured by cloud, this is known as sheet lightning.

Upper atmospheric
This type of lightning occurs far above thunderstorms. It includes red sprites, which flicker and dance in the air. It is usually faint and cannot be seen from the ground.

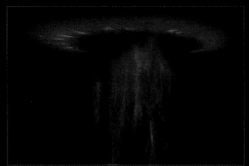

Survivors' stories

Eight out of every ten people struck by lightning survive. However, many survivors have problems afterwards. These include stiff joints, blindness or sensitivity to light, hearing loss, memory loss, insomnia (inability to sleep), chronic pain, and difficulty sitting still for long periods at a time.

Struck seven times
US park ranger Roy Sullivan was struck by lightning a record-breaking seven times in 35 years – each time living to tell the tale.

Sparking a wildfire

Sparks from a bolt of lightning start a fire on the dry grasslands of South Africa. Minutes later, rain from the stormclouds extinguishes the fire before it can spread. Lightning is one of the main causes of wildfires.

How it works

In a thunderstorm, water droplets in the clouds collide, giving them an electric charge. The charge builds up until there is a flash of lightning, which connects the negative charges in the cloud to positive charges on the ground.

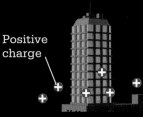

Negative charge

Positive charge

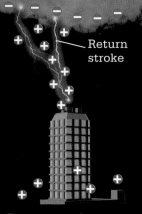

Stepped leader stroke

Return stroke

220,000,000 kph
(145,400,000 mph): average speed of a
lightning bolt

1 Charge builds up
Negative charges at the base of a thundercloud attract positive charges from the ground.

2 Leader stroke
Moving in short steps, a channel of negative charges called a stepped leader stroke zigzags its way to the ground.

3 Return stroke
When the negative and positive charges connect, lightning flashes back up to the cloud.

Big freeze [Killer cold]

When the temperature drops, rain can be replaced by ice and snow. Snow looks beautiful, but the cold can kill. If the temperature falls below −15°C (5°F), people caught outside risk frostbite or may even die of hypothermia.

Snowstorms and blizzards

Snowstorms form when freezing polar air meets warmer, more moist air. The heavier cold air forces the moist, warm air upwards, where it condenses into clouds and snow. A snowstorm becomes a blizzard when winds reach over 56 kph (35 mph) and visibility is less than 400 m (1,300 ft).

Cold air | Warm air
SNOW | SLEET | FREEZING RAIN | RAIN

Snow, sleet, or rain
Snow falls if cloud-to-ground air remains cold. If air near the ground is warmer, the snow melts into sleet or freezing rain as it falls.

Lightening the load
Firefighters dig a house out of snow in a Romanian village in 2012. The same cold spell killed over 500 people in eastern Europe, bringing snow of up to 5 m (16.5 ft) deep.

World blizzards

In severe blizzards, icy winds whip snow along at speeds of more than 72 kph (45 mph), and visibility is reduced to zero. Blizzards are common in the United States, Canada, and Russia, and they also occur in other mountainous countries, such as Iran and Afghanistan.

1888

USA and Canada
In March 1888, the Great Blizzard dropped 1.3 m (4 ft) of snow over the eastern United States and Canada. Icy winds piled the snow into record-breaking drifts, some up to 15 m (50 ft) high. Over 400 people died.

1927

Russia
Temperatures fell to −40°C (−40°F) as one of the century's worst blizzards struck Moscow and western Siberia.

Dead end
Workers try to free a train trapped between walls of snow in New York, USA, in 1888.

When cold kills

To work properly, your body temperature needs to stay at a steady 37°C (98.6°F). If it falls below this for too long, the result may be hypothermia.

37°C (98.6°F)
Normal body temperature

36°C (96.8°F)
Reduced body temperature:
Shivering

35°C (95.0°F)
Mild hypothermia:
Strange behaviour

32°C (89.6°F)
Moderate hypothermia:
Difficulty moving

28°C (82.4°F)
Severe hypothermia:
Loss of consciousness; possibly death

1972

Iran
Around 4,000 people died during the deadliest blizzard on record. Winds dumped as much as 8 m (26 ft) of snow on some villages, burying all of the inhabitants.

1993

USA and Canada
This blizzard was nicknamed the "Storm of the Century" because of its huge snowfalls and hurricane-force winds. It killed over 300 people, mainly due to hypothermia.

2008

Afghanistan
During this blizzard, nearly 1,000 people died in mountainous parts of the country, as up to 2 m (6.5 ft) of snow fell and temperatures dropped as low as −25°C (−13°F).

Danger above

Icicles form when drops of water freeze, eventually creating long spikes of ice. They can be dangerous when they break off rooftops. In Russia, falling icicles kill dozens of people every year.

Spears of ice
Icicles can be over 1 m (3 ft) long. They are more stable in freezing weather but may fall when the air warms up.

Avalanche! [White death]

Snow may look harmless, but it can kill if it suddenly starts to slide downhill. Within seconds, it can move at up to 130 kph (80 mph), burying anything in its path.

90% of avalanches
that involve people are triggered by the victim or someone nearby

Types of avalanche

No two avalanches are exactly the same. Some happen when powdery snow starts to slide. Others are triggered when a layer under packed snow suddenly gives way. All types of avalanche are most common in early spring, when warm air melts and loosens packed snow.

Release point
These avalanches often start from a point like a tree.

Loose snow
Loose, powdery snow starts to roll down a slope in a widening fan shape.

Wind direction

Fracture zone

Overhanging snow

Giant slabs
Chunks can be the size of cars.

Cornice
Snow, blown by the wind, builds up on a ridge. The overhanging snow then breaks at the fracture zone, tumbling down the slope below.

Slab
An entire layer of snow begins to move, breaking up into pieces as it heads downhill.

Protection

Skiers and snowboarders are warned if there is a risk of an avalanche. Villages are protected through blasting and by erecting barriers.

Blasting
Explosives dislodge snow in a controlled way.

Barriers
Netting and wooden barriers can stop small snowslides.

Survival

Carrying the right equipment can save your life or help you rescue another person. A survival pack contains an inflatable air bag and a shovel for use if you are trapped in snow. A probe locates victims, so that rescuers know where to dig.

Avalanche kit
The transceiver broadcasts a radio signal. When set to receive mode, it can pinpoint the signal of someone who is buried in snow.

Folding probe

Folding shovel

Transceiver

Rescue

Speed is vital in a rescue, because the chance of survival falls rapidly after just 15 minutes. Dogs can tell people where to dig.

Dogs on duty
Trained dogs can locate the scent of someone trapped under 2 m (6.5 feet) of snow.

Eyewitness

NAME: Ian Measeck

DATE: 27 February 2010

LOCATION: New York State, USA

DETAILS: Ian Measeck of Glens Falls was caught in an avalanche while skiing down Wright Peak.

❝ The sensation is best described as almost instant acceleration in a river of wet cement. I was suddenly surrounded by this flowing snowbank. . . . I don't remember much aside from the dark, the fear, and the thought that I had to try to stay on top of it somehow. ❞

Tumbling snow
Visitors at the Mount Foraker base camp in Denali National Park, in Alaska, watch snow tumble down the mountainside.

Locked in ice

If rain falls through cold air, it sometimes freezes as it lands, draping trees and power lines with icicles and coating roads in a slippery glaze. Although they are beautiful, ice storms can be deadly. This ice storm killed more than 50 people in the American Midwest in 2009.

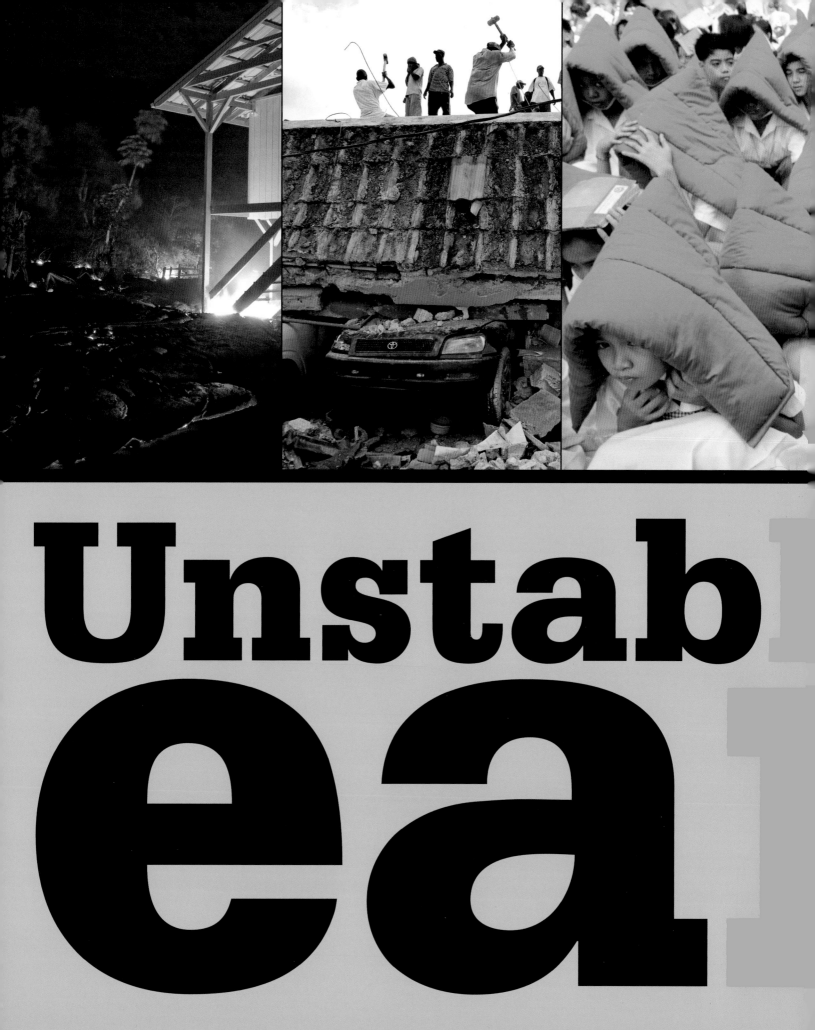

Unstab

eat

* What is pahoehoe lava?

* Which country's capital was flattened in 2010?

* How can you survive an earthquake?

Landslides [Shifting

We take solid ground for granted, but disaster can strike if it starts to slip and slide. Some landslides are slow and gradual. The most dangerous happen quickly, without warning, making it difficult to escape.

Cause and effect

Frost and rain often help loosen slopes, making soil unstable. People also cause landslides, by cutting down trees that have roots holding the earth in place. Some landslides are caused by earthquakes or volcanic activity (see pages 58–59).

Types of movement

Landslides range from slow soil creep to rockfalls in which forces holding a slope together suddenly give way.

Soil creep
Soil slowly edges downhill as it freezes and thaws.

Slumping
The ground slides in curved slabs, forming giant terraces, or steps.

Debris slide
Rocks shattered by frost race down the side of a mountain.

Mudflow
Mud pours downhill after a heavy rain.

Rockfall
Rocks plummet through the air as a slope collapses.

The fastest landslides move at
5 metres (15 feet) a second!

Mudslide disasters

Steep slopes and crowded housing can be a dangerous mix. During storms, heavy rain can start to move the soil in a muddy mass that overwhelms anything (or anybody) in its path as it sweeps downhill.

CHINA, AUGUST 2010 – 1,000+ KILLED

GUATEMALA, SEPTEMBER 2010 – 50 KILLED

BRAZIL, JANUARY 2011 – 900+ KILLED

Giant rockfall

Watched by a solitary figure, a giant rockfall crashes into a valley in northeast Pakistan in January 2010. A few weeks earlier, an even larger landslide in the same area blocked the River Hunza. It formed a new lake that flooded farmland and submerged villages, forcing 30,000 people to move.

Restless Earth

Many of the world's worst disasters happen because Earth's crust is on the move. Little by little, huge blocks of crust called plates collide or separate, causing earthquakes and volcanic eruptions where they meet or pull apart.

Types of boundaries

At transform boundaries, Earth's plates grind past each other, causing earthquakes. At divergent boundaries, the plates pull apart, and at convergent boundaries, they collide. Diverging and converging often result in volcanic activity.

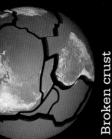

Mobile crust

The crust, or outer layer of Earth, is split into giant plates. These "float" on the magma, or molten rock, below. Magma flows like thick tar, moving the plates about 3–4 cm (1–1.5 ins) a year.

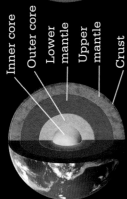

Inner core
Outer core
Lower mantle
Upper mantle
Crust

Moving plates
Magma pushed up from the mantle creates new crust that moves plates at divergent boundaries.

Broken crust
The plates carry land, ocean, or both. They meet at fault lines.

56 cm (2 ins) average yearly movement of the San Andreas Fault

San Andreas Fault
This fault lies on the boundary between the Pacific plate and the North American plate.

NORTH AMERICAN PLATE

UNITED STATES

SOUTH AMERICAN PLATE

CHILE

Ring of Fire
The world's most active fault surrounds the Pacific plate in a "ring of fire". The plate has active volcanoes all along its edge.

90% of all earthquakes occur around the **Pacific Ring of Fire**

PACIFIC PLATE

NEW ZEALAND

EURASIAN PLATE

INDO-AUSTRALIAN PLATE

AFRICAN PLATE

ICELAND

ANTARCTIC PLATE

KEY
● Significant volcanoes

Mid-Atlantic Ridge

Fault lines
Fault lines mark the giant cracks in Earth's surface where plates are pushed up, sink down, or move sideways.

World plates
There are 7 large plates and about 40 smaller ones. This map shows the world's main plates.

Eyjafjallajökull eruption
The country of Iceland lies on the Mid-Atlantic Ridge, where two plates are diverging, or pulling apart. Volcanic activity, such as the eruption of Eyjafjallajökull in 2010, is common at divergent boundaries.

Christchurch earthquake
Parts of New Zealand lie over transform boundaries, where two plates may suddenly slip or slide past each other. The 2011 earthquake in Christchurch, New Zealand, killed over 180 people.

Chaitén volcanic eruption
In 2009, the eruption of Mount Chaitén, in Chile, coated a nearby town in a thick layer of ash. Like many volcanoes, it lies close to a convergent boundary, where two plates are colliding head-on.

Yellowstone geyser
Despite being far from a boundary or a fault line, Yellowstone's springs and geysers are heated by "hot spots". Magma rises to just below the surface, making a bulge and causing volcanic activity.

Sea and land collide

Deep below the oceans, rising magma at divergent plate boundaries constantly makes new seabed. Like a slow-motion conveyor belt, the seabed spreads sideways toward convergent boundaries, where it is forced below plates that carry land.

Volcanoes form
Mountains and volcanoes grow as the land is pushed up at the plate's edge.

Seabed spreads
The seabed on each side of the ridge spreads apart as new crust is made.

Plates collide
The converging plate carrying the dense seabed is pushed beneath the lighter land-bearing plate.

Colliding plates
At convergent boundaries, the heavier crust carrying the seabed buckles and partly melts as it is forced below the more lightweight land-bearing plate. This violent collision produces powerful earthquakes. Upwellings of magma at the plate edges may also form volcanoes.

Seabed forms
The hot rock solidifies as it meets the cooler ocean waters.

Magma emerges
The magma wells up through a fault line at a mid-ocean ridge.

Magma rises
Currents of magma slowly rise from the depths of the mantle.

Geologists, or earth scientists, are on the frontline of research about natural disasters. Some risk their lives to study active volcanoes. Others investigate earthquakes to learn how and when they may next strike.

Seismologists

Seismologists study all kinds of earthquakes, from tiny ground tremors to huge jolts. One of their jobs is to examine the way that forces build up below the ground before quakes occur. This may help them warn people that a quake is going to hit.

Telltale trace
This trace from a seismograph (see page 49) shows ground movement during a quake.

Parkfield case study

The town of Parkfield, California, sits right on top of the San Andreas Fault (see page 44). Bristling with seismological instruments, it is the best-studied earthquake zone in the world. At Parkfield, scientists measure the way that the ground creeps along the fault, where two neighbouring plates meet.

San Andreas Fault
Seen from the air, the San Andreas Fault looks like a gigantic scar slicing across the land. In this view, near Parkfield, the edge of the Pacific plate is on the left, and the edge of the North American plate is on the right.

Laser monitoring
At Parkfield, instruments called geodimeters aim laser beams across the fault. The beams bounce back from reflectors, and computers measure how long they take to return. Any change in time taken is caused by movement in the rocks along the fault.

Creep meter
A creep meter calculates fault slip (how the rocks move in relation to one another). The meter measures the distance between two piers placed in the ground. The piers are connected by a wire. Any movements in the wire are measured by electronic gauges.

Strainmeter
Strainmeters monitor tiny deformations in the Earth's crust due to fault slips, earthquakes, and volcanic activity. Powered by solar panels, strainmeters can be completely automatic. They send data to satellites, and the data is then transmitted to computers on Earth for analysis.

Dancing with death

A volcanologist records lava flowing from Mount Etna, on the Italian island of Sicily. When it solidifies, the lava will form the black rock that surrounds the flow. Etna is the largest active volcano in Europe, and one of the world's most studied volcanoes.

Volcanologists at work

Volcanologists are like detectives. They track down clues from volcanic rocks or gases to predict future eruptions and perhaps save lives. Their work sometimes takes them right to the edge of an exploding volcano, where dangers may include inhaling poisonous gas or being injured by red-hot lava.

In the field

In a protective suit that reflects heat, a scientist uses a pickaxe to take a sample of lava back to the laboratory for analysis.

Radar gun

A volcanologist uses a radar gun to measure the speed of lava flow beneath surface rocks. The gun is similar to those used to measure the speed of a baseball as it is pitched.

Earthquakes happen with little warning, so there is almost no time for people to react. For a few terrifying minutes, the ground shakes violently, sometimes bringing buildings crashing down.

Types of earthquake

Earthquakes occur along faults in Earth's crust, at plate margins. If neighbouring plates move or get stuck, energy builds up until it is finally released in an earthquake.

Normal faults
These are found at divergent boundaries, where one plate drops relative to the other. Resulting earthquakes vary in strength. One along the Mid-Atlantic Ridge in 2011 reached magnitude 5.2.

Thrust faults
These are found at convergent boundaries, where one plate is pushed below the other. The result is an earthquake and sometimes a tsunami. This happened in Chile in 1960.

Epicentre
Most damage occurs at the epicentre – the point directly above the hypocentre.

Seismic waves
These waves of energy spread out from the hypocentre.

Hypocentre
The hypocentre, or focus, is where the rock fractures.

Strike-slip faults
These are found at transform boundaries, where one plate slides past another. The result can range from minor tremors to a huge earthquake, such as the one in Haiti in 2010.

Twisted tracks
Workers assess damage to a railroad track after a huge earthquake hit Christchurch, New Zealand, in 2010.

The Richter scale

The Richter scale measures an earthquake's magnitude, or intensity. Each step up represents a tenfold increase, so a quake that measures 8 shakes the ground 1,000 times more than a quake that measures 5.

MAGNITUDE CHART

9 Extreme
Major damage and death (1 every 10 years)

8 Great
Serious damage over extensive area (1 per year)

7 Major
Serious damage over large area (1 per month)

6 Strong
Great damage near epicentre (10 per month)

5 Moderate
Some damage near epicentre (100 per month)

4 Light
Usually felt, damage rare (over 1 per hour)

3 Minor
Felt near epicentre only, damage rare (10 per hour)

0–2 Micro
Not felt, no damage (over 100 per hour)

9.0
8.0
7.0
6.0
5.0
4.0
3.0
2.0
1.0

Measuring quakes

Seismographs measure the magnitude of an earthquake by sensing the ground's movement. They can pick up tremors from an earthquake on the opposite side of Earth.

Seismograph
In this device, ink traces seismic waves onto a roll of paper.

Magnitude 9.5: the most powerful earthquake ever recorded on Earth, in Chile, on 22 May 1960

9.1
Indonesia, 2004
This earthquake below the seabed triggered a huge tsunami (see pages 74–75).

7.9
China, 2008
The Sichuan earthquake was followed by over 100 smaller earthquakes, or aftershocks.

7.0
Haiti, 2010
Although not the strongest known earthquake to hit Haiti, this was by far the deadliest (see pages 50–51).

Deadly earthquakes

Throughout history, earthquakes striking populated regions have killed millions of people. On the other hand, the most powerful earthquake ever recorded, in Chile in 1960, caused fewer deaths (around 5,000) because it struck an area with a low population.

526 CE	**Antakya, Turkey**	250,000 killed; magnitude unknown
865 CE	**Damghan, Iran**	200,000 killed; magnitude unknown
1138	**Aleppo, Syria**	230,000 killed; magnitude unknown
1290	**Chihli, China**	100,000 killed; magnitude unknown
1556	**Shaanxi, China**	830,000 killed; magnitude 8
1727	**Tabriz, Iran**	77,000 killed; magnitude 7.7
1908	**Messina, Italy**	72,000 killed; magnitude 7.5
1920	**Gansu, China**	200,000 killed; magnitude 7.8
1923	**Kanto, Japan**	142,800 killed; magnitude 7.9
1948	**Ashkhabad, Turkmenistan**	110,000 killed; magnitude 7.3
1976	**Tangshan, China**	242,769 killed; magnitude 7.5
2004	**Sumatra, Indonesia**	227,898 killed; magnitude 9.1
2008	**Sichuan, China**	87,587 killed; magnitude 7.9
2010	**Port-au-Prince, Haiti**	316,000 killed; magnitude 7.0

Aftermath of an earthquake

In January 2010, a catastrophic earthquake hit Haiti, one of the poorest nations in the world. It devastated Haiti's capital city of Port-au-Prince, home to 2 million people, triggering an international rescue effort.

12 JAN. (4:53 PM)
Earthquake epicentre
Pressure building up in the rocks along a strike-slip fault (see page 48) was suddenly released in a massive earthquake. The quake struck near the town of Léogâne, 25 km (16 miles) west of Port-au-Prince.

Port-au-Prince

HAITI

Léogâne

12 JAN.
Buildings destroyed
As dusk approached, people dug through rubble with their bare hands, trying to rescue survivors. Around 70 percent of the city's buildings had collapsed, including 4,000 schools.

SEARCHING THROUGH THE DEBRIS

13 JAN.
Rescue teams from Cuba and Peru started to arrive; staff at remaining hospitals struggled to treat the wounded.

14 JAN.
People used social networking sites, such as Facebook and Twitter, to raise money to help rescue operations.

16 JAN.
Temporary hospitals were set up, including Red Cross basic healthcare units.

12/1   13/1   15/1   16/1

15 JAN.
Eighteen-month-old baby Winnie was found alive, after being trapped for 68 hours inside a collapsed building.

17 JAN.
Panic set in when two aftershocks, measuring 4.6 and 4.7, struck 16 km (10 miles) west of Port-au-Prince.

12 JAN.
Huge casualties
First reports said that 200,000 people had been killed, and many more injured. Most of the city's hospitals were destroyed. Rubble-filled streets made it impossible to distribute food, water, and medicine.

15 JAN.
Search and rescue
Teams from more than 20 countries were now working to find survivors. Ships and planes started to bring in food and clean drinking water.

WOMAN RESCUED FROM THE RUBBLE

Monique Clesca, Port-au-Prince, 12 January:
"I saw a cloud of dust rise as whole neighbourhoods fell like popcorn"

[Haiti]

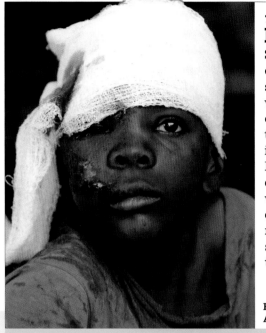

18 JAN.
Medical aid
Six days after the earthquake, Médecins sans Frontières (Doctors without Borders) had established four treatment facilities in Port-au-Prince. However, thousands of people were still waiting for medical care and living in makeshift tent cities scattered across the capital.

HAITIAN CHILD IN A TENT HOSPITAL

FRENCH RESCUE TEAM

27 JAN.
Girl rescued alive
Exhausted and dehydrated, yet still alive 15 days after the earthquake struck, 16-year-old Darlene Étienne was rescued from the rubble. She had survived by drinking water from a bathtub.

20 JAN.
US Navy hospital ship USNS Comfort *began to receive injured patients from local hospitals.*

USNS *COMFORT*

18/1 • • 20/1 • • 23/1 • • • 27/1 • • • 2011

20 JAN.
An aftershock, measuring 5.9, caused weakened buildings to collapse.

23 JAN.
The Haitian government declared search-and-rescue efforts over.

30 JAN.
A food distribution programme was set up by the United Nations.

Aftermath
The struggle to help the people of Haiti continued.

18 JAN.
Emergency supplies
The US Air Force began to deliver aid packages to designated areas in the countryside surrounding the capital city.

PARACHUTE AIRDROP

2011
One year later
A year after the earthquake, Haiti was still on the long road to recovery. About 1 million people were living in tents, and only 5 percent of the rubble blocking the streets of Port-au-Prince had been cleared.

TENT CITY IN PORT-AU-PRINCE

Living with earthquakes

Scientists can detect earthquakes, but they still cannot predict when or where the next big one will strike. That is why it is important to be prepared when you live in, or are visiting, an earthquake zone.

Taipei 101 tower

Earthquake prediction

The first earthquake detector was made in China, in 132 CE. It showed that a quake had occurred, and in which direction. Modern seismometers are much more precise. Working in groups, they pinpoint earthquakes thousands of kilometres away.

Dragon releases ball in quake

Ancient detector
This Chinese detector contained eight bronze balls. When it shook, one of the dragons dropped a ball into the frog's open mouth below.

Modern seismometer
Some digital seismometers are designed for use on the seabed, where an earthquake may cause a tsunami (see page 72).

Building protection

Some of the world's tallest buildings stand in earthquake zones. They are protected from damage during an earthquake by shock-absorbing foundations and tuned mass dampers, which work like giant pendulums.

101 pendulum
The pendulum at the top of the tower swings during tremors or strong winds, absorbing energy that could otherwise make the building collapse.

Taipei 101
This record-breaking building is over 500 m (1,640 ft) tall. Its main pendulum, suspended between the 87th and 92nd floors, weighs as much as two fully loaded jumbo jets.

prepared]

he average number of people who die
n earthquakes every year

More here
For key to symbols, see page 112

Into the Firestorm: A Novel of San Francisco, 1906
by Deborah Hopkinson

Visit a museum to find out more about earthquakes. The **Natural History Museum** in London, UK, has a re-creation of a Japanese supermarket that shows how it was shaken and damaged during the Kobe earthquake in 1995.

Find out where earthquakes are occurring all over the world right now at http://earthquake.usgs.gov/earthquakes/recenteqsww.

Follow these rules if you are caught inside during an earthquake:
- Drop to the ground.
- Take cover under a strong desk or table.
- Hold on until the shaking stops.

seismometer: an instrument that records vibrations produced by earthquakes.

tremor: a shaking or vibrating movement of the earth during an earthquake.

tuned mass damper: a heavy weight mounted in skyscrapers and other buildings to protect them during an earthquake.

Eyewitness
NAME: Ryosuke
DATE: 11 March 2011
LOCATION: Tokyo, Japan
DETAILS: Office worker Ryosuke posted this online shortly after the Tohoku earthquake struck off the Japanese coast (see pages 76–77).

❝ Although we're far from northern Japan, the quake here was very big. The first quake was very long – everyone in the office was screaming. Then we had another long one about 30 minutes after that. Paper and items were falling off the desks. . . . We can hear the walls going back and forth. ❞

Earthquake drill
In the Philippine capital of Manila, children cover their heads with padded hoods as part of an earthquake drill. The Philippines lies on the Pacific Ring of Fire – the most earthquake-prone region in the world (see pages 44–45).

Red-hot river

On the island of Hawaii, a river of red-hot lava from Kilauea volcano creeps forward at a rate of around 800 metres (2,600 feet) per hour. Although this house's owner had enough time to escape, he was unable to keep his wooden home from catching on fire.

Stratovolcanoes

While you are reading this, about 20 volcanoes are erupting somewhere around the world. The most dangerous kinds are giant stratovolcanoes, which can blast ash and gas high into Earth's atmosphere.

Life cycle of a volcano

Most active stratovolcanoes are less than 100,000 years old. A stratovolcano is particularly dangerous during the first part of its life cycle, when it can reach a gigantic size. Eventually, its eruptions become less frequent. Finally, they stop altogether, and the volcano becomes extinct.

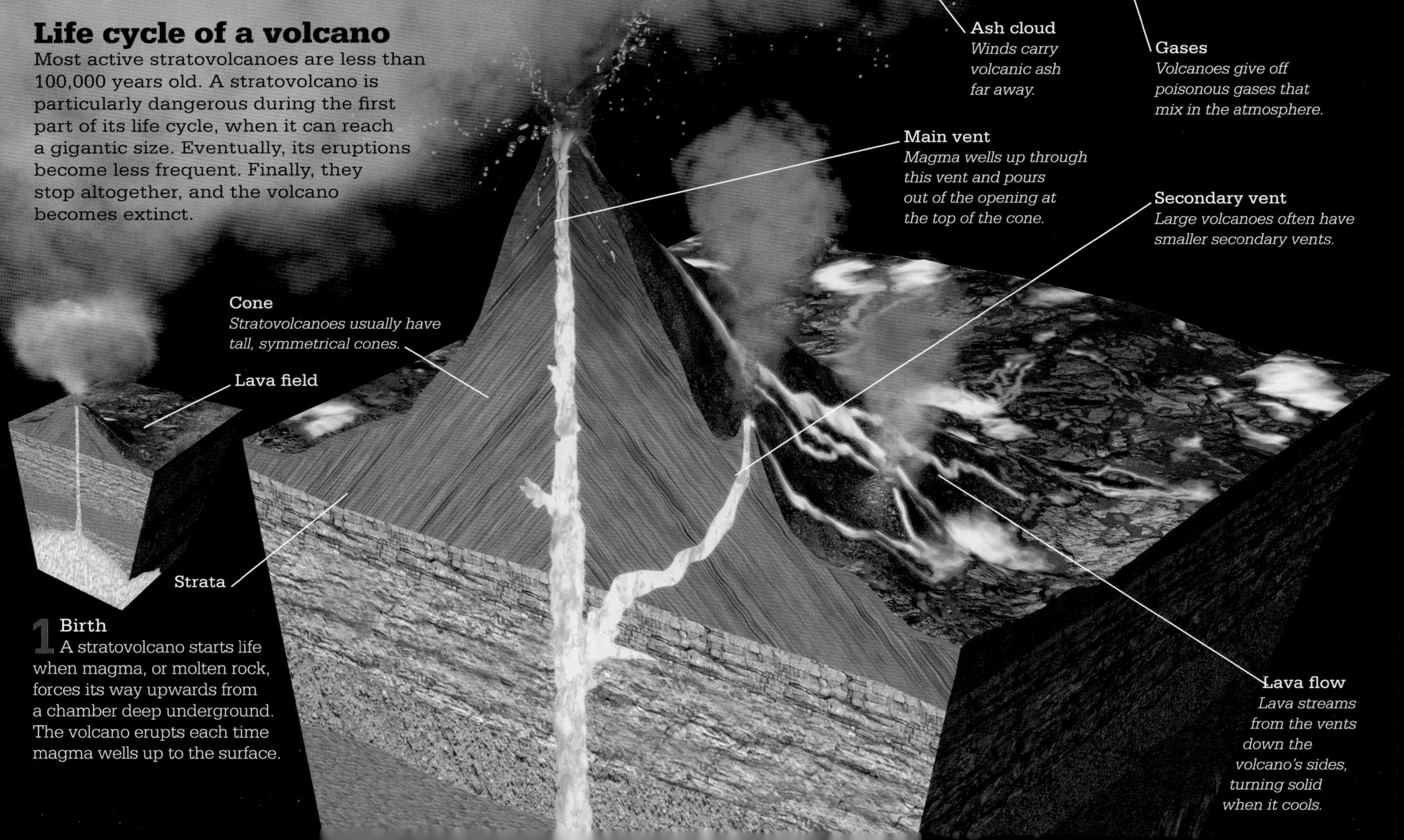

Gases
Volcanoes give off poisonous gases that mix in the atmosphere.

Ash cloud
Winds carry volcanic ash far away.

Secondary vent
Large volcanoes often have smaller secondary vents.

Main vent
Magma wells up through this vent and pours out of the opening at the top of the cone.

Lava flow
Lava streams from the vents down the volcano's sides, turning solid when it cools.

Cone
Stratovolcanoes usually have tall, symmetrical cones.

Lava field

Strata

1 Birth
A stratovolcano starts life when magma, or molten rock, forces its way upwards from a chamber deep underground. The volcano erupts each time magma wells up to the surface.

Conduit
This passageway connects the magma chamber to the volcano's vents.

Vesuvius eruption
In 79 CE, Mount Vesuvius suddenly erupted in Italy, covering the nearby cities of Herculaneum and Pompeii in a 4-m (13-ft) layer of burning pumice and ash.

Victim of Pompeii
The buried cities were rediscovered in 1748. This plaster cast of a body shape, left beneath hardened ash after the body rotted away, shows the victim's terror.

Lava field

Eroded cone

Plug of solid magma

2 Active period
Layers of ash and lava, called strata, form with each eruption, building up into a tall, steep-sided cone. The volcano grows rapidly, until it may be over 5,000 m (16,400 ft) high. A field of lava spreads out from its base, creating a desolate landscape with few signs of life.

Magma

Magma chamber
Molten rock is kept liquid by Earth's internal heat.

3 Erosion
When the volcano is no longer active, erosion takes over. Wind and rain eat away at the hardened ash, and the cone and the lava field shrink in size. Plants grow in cracks in the lava, nourished by the fertile volcanic soil.

4 Volcanic plug
After many thousands of years, the lava field is still visible, but most of the cone has eroded away. The only part left is a tall "plug" – the core of hardened magma from the volcano's main conduit.

Volcanic fallout
When a volcano erupts, billions of rocky particles are blasted into the air. The heaviest fragments soon drop to the ground, but specks of ash can be blown great distances by strong winds.

Ash particle
Sharp edges are dangerous if ash gets into eyes or aeroplane engines.

Ash
Particles of ash are less than 2 mm (0.08 inches) across. A dense ash cloud can blot out the Sun.

Lapilli
Measuring 2–64 mm (0.08–2.5 ins) across, lapilli look like tiny stones. They turn from molten to solid rock as they fall.

Bombs
Fragments over 64 mm (2.5 ins) drop near the vent.

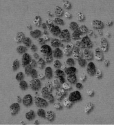

Lava and lahars

When volcanoes erupt, molten rock pouring down their slopes can crush and set fire to buildings. Almost as dangerous are lahars – rivers of volcanic mud – which set like concrete once they stop flowing.

Lava on the move

A huge lava flow cascaded from Nyiragongo, a volcano in central Africa, in 2002. It ploughed through the nearby city of Goma, destroying over 4,000 buildings. Fortunately, most of the people in danger had enough time to escape.

Types of lava

Pahoehoe lava is thin and runny, with a glassy skin. It forms a smooth surface when it cools and becomes solid. Aa lava is stickier than pahoehoe lava and has a rough surface when it solidifies. Pillow lava forms on the seabed like toothpaste being squeezed out of a tube. Lava bombs are lumps of molten rock, thrown up into the air during an eruption on land.

PAHOEHOE LAVA

AA LAVA

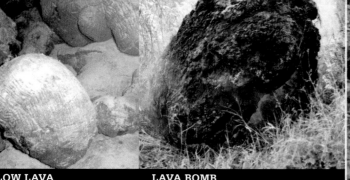

PILLOW LAVA   LAVA BOMB

and mud]

Rocky river

This boy, standing in the centre of the ruined town of Goma, is holding a lump of cooled lava from the explosion. Behind him, Nyiragongo volcano continues to send out clouds of smoke and ash.

Volcanic lahars

Thick, heavy, and full of sharp-edged particles, lahars are triggered by volcanic eruptions or heavy rain. Once the muddy mixture has loosened from the hillside, it pours down in a grey torrent, engulfing fields and homes. In 1991, the eruption of Mount Pinatubo, followed by a hurricane, triggered lahars in the Philippines.

Rooftop rescue

Surrounded by a sea of thick mud, Filipino schoolchildren wait to be rescued. Luckily, most people had time to escape to safety.

More here

For key to symbols, see page 112

hot spot volcanic winter volcanic vent **tephra black smoker** caldera pyroclastic flow **geyser fumarole**

Volcanoes: Journey to the Crater's Edge
by Robert Burleigh and Philippe Bourseiller

Witness to Disaster: Volcanoes
by Judy and Dennis Fradin

"NeMO Dive!"
http://www.pmel.noaa.gov/vents/nemo/dive.html

"Hawai'i Volcanoes Webcams"
http://www.nps.gov/havo/photosmultimedia/webcams.htm

"Volcanoes 101"
http://video.nationalgeographic.com/video/kids/forces-of-nature-kids/volcanoes-101-kids/

Visit the **Thomas A. Jaggar Museum** in Hawai'i Volcanoes National Park to see seismographs and special volcanologist gear.

Start your own collection of volcanic rocks by visiting volcanic areas or buying specimens from shops that specialize in minerals and fossils.

Volcano facts and stats

Volcanoes are the world's scariest mountains – and some of the biggest. There are around 500 active volcanoes on Earth, and many more are either dormant (inactive) or extinct. And appearances can be deceiving. After thousands of years in a deep "sleep", dormant volcanoes can suddenly erupt, bringing disaster to those living nearby.

Fastest-growing volcano

In February 1943, a new volcano burst to life in a cornfield in Mexico. The volcano was named Parícutin, after a nearby village, and became the fastest-growing volcano ever recorded, soon towering above the surrounding landscape.

After 9 years
By the time it stopped erupting, Parícutin had grown to 424 m (1,391 ft).

After 1 year
After a year of continual eruptions, Parícutin was 336 m (1,102 ft) tall.

After 1 day
Within 24 hours, Parícutin's cinder cone was 50 m (164 ft) tall.

Statue of Liberty
The statue measures 93 m (305 ft) from torch to ground.

Loudest noise

In 1883, the volcanic island of Krakatau, between Java and Sumatra in Indonesia, exploded. The eruption produced the loudest sound ever recorded – thousands of times louder than a space shuttle launch.

KRAKATAU

Hear this
The explosion of Krakatau could be heard in Perth, Australia, over 3,540 km (2,200 miles) away.

Perth

AUSTRALIA

4.5 hours: the time it took the sound of the explosion to travel from Krakatau to Australia

Volcano states

Volcanoes are categorized as active, dormant, or extinct. A dormant volcano can become active again, but an extinct volcano has reached the end of its active life and is unlikely to erupt again.

Active
These may erupt, emit gas, or produce ground tremors.

Dormant
These are inactive, but may have erupted in the last 10,000 years.

Extinct
These are inactive, and have not erupted in the last 10,000 years.

Volcano shapes

Volcanoes have different shapes, depending on the types of lava that they produce. Stratovolcanoes and cinder cones are built up from thick, slow-moving, sticky lava. Shield volcanoes are formed from thin, runny lava, which flows a long way before it becomes solid.

Common types
These outlines show three main volcanic shapes. Cinder cones are the most common type of volcano.

Stratovolcano
This type has a tall, steep-sided cone, built up from layers of lava and ash.

Shield volcano
This is dome-shaped, with wide, gently sloping sides.

Cinder cone
This has a wide, steep-sided crater, mostly built up from layers of lapilli (see page 57).

Most deadly volcanoes

Indonesia has the greatest number of active volcanoes in the world. Of the ten highest death tolls from volcanoes in history, five followed eruptions in Indonesia.

3,500 VESUVIUS (ITALY) 1631
10

5,000 KELUT (INDONESIA) 1919
8

4,000 GALUNGGUNG (INDONESIA) 1882
9

9,000 LAKI (ICELAND) 1783
7

10,000 KELUT (INDONESIA) 1586
6

15,000 UNZEN (JAPAN) 1792
5

25,000 NEVADO DEL RUIZ (COLOMBIA) 1985
4

29,000 MONT PELÉE (MARTINIQUE) 1902
3

36,000 KRAKATAU (INDONESIA) 1883
2

92,000 TAMBORA (INDONESIA) 1815
1

Death toll

The highest number of known deaths from an eruption occurred in 1815, when Mount Tambora exploded in Indonesia. People died in the eruption itself, or from famine after ash smothered farm animals and crops.

146 cubic km: (35 cubic miles)
the amount of ash that Tambora ejected into the atmosphere

Biggest volcanoes

The biggest volcano in our solar system is Olympus Mons on Mars. This enormous shield volcano could easily swallow up the ten biggest volcanoes on Earth, with room to spare. The tallest volcano on Earth, measured from sea level, is Ojos del Salado, which is part of the Andes mountain chain in South America.

Highest mountain
Mount Everest is not a volcano, but it is the world's tallest mountain. It stands around 2,000 m (6,500 ft) higher than Ojos del Salado.

Martian giant
Olympus Mons is nearly three timeas taller than Mount Everest.

Earth's tallest volcanoes
On land, Earth's tallest volcano is Ojos del Salado. However, if measured from their bases on the seafloor, the tallest volcanoes are Mauna Kea and neighbouring Mauna Loa on the island of Hawaii.

Highest from seafloor
Mauna Kea and Mauna Loa rise over 10,000 m (32,800 ft) from the seafloor.

OLYMPUS MONS 25,000 M (82,000 FT)

Highest volcano
Ojos del Salado is a stratovolcano located on the border between Argentina and Chile.

Volcanic island
Mauna Kea is a huge shield volcano on the island of Hawaii.

MOUNT EVEREST 8,848 M (29,029 FT)

OJOS DEL SALADO 6,893 M (22,615 FT)

MAUNA KEA 4,205 M (13,796 FT)

MAUNA LOA 4,169 M (13,678 FT)

Sea level

Ground gives way
On 30 May 2010, a hole as big as a 20-storey building appeared in Guatemala City, swallowing roads and buildings. It formed when volcanic ash deep underground suddenly collapsed after becoming saturated with water. Amazingly, this disaster caused only one known death.

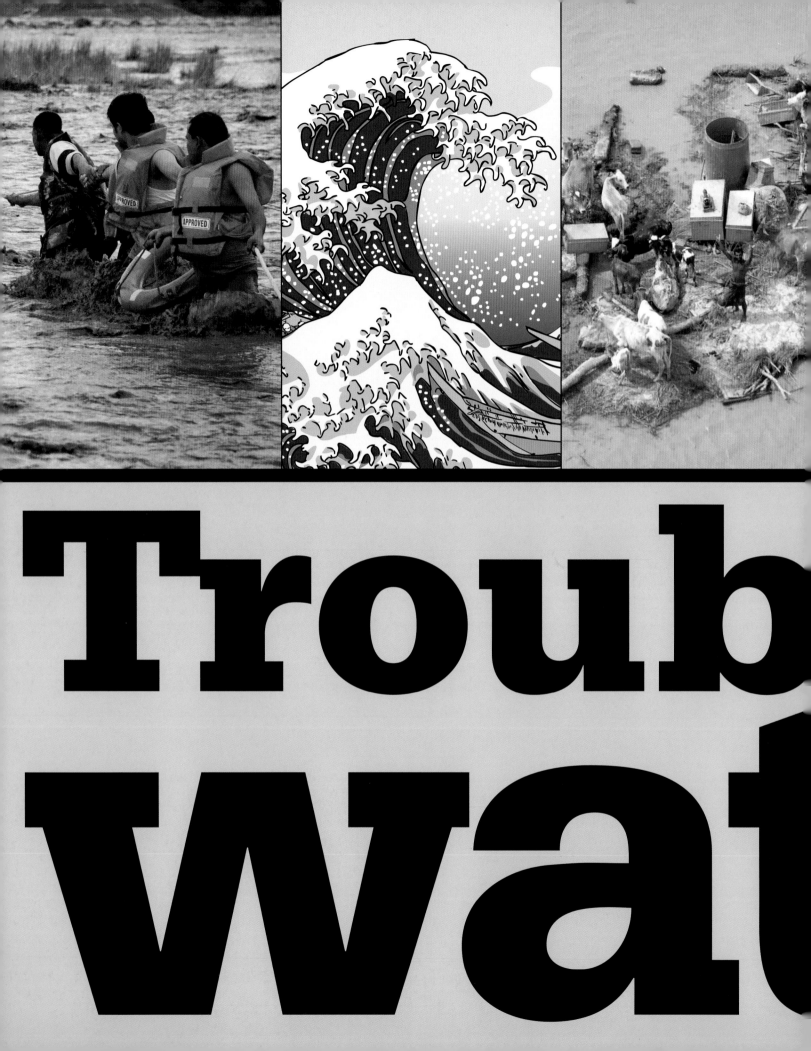

Troub
wat

* Where was the worst flood?

* Which giant wave killed around 230,000 people?

* Which continent suffers the most extreme monsoons?

Flooding [Water running wild]

Floods kill around 20,000 people worldwide every year. Most floods occur after prolonged and heavy rain, when waterlogged ground can no longer absorb any more water.

Around the world

In 2010, flooding brought disaster all over the world. Many people drowned in torrential rain or flash floods; others were buried when saturated ground gave way and engulfed homes in landslides or mudslides. The worst floods occurred in Pakistan, where heavy monsoon rains flooded one-fifth of the country (see pages 68–69).

Portugal

In February, extreme storms brought torrential rain to Funchal, the capital of the Portuguese island of Madeira, causing water to suddenly surge downhill in a flash flood. More than 40 people were killed.

United States

Heavy rain in June caused flooding across 60 of Nebraska's 93 counties, including the region where the River Platte flows into the Missouri. Both rivers burst their banks, flooding land for kilometres around and submerging homes and farms. This caused $14 million in damage.

Colombia

An unusually heavy wet season, with torrential rainfall, affected 70 percent of the country, hidden here under a giant storm system. Around 300 people were killed, and 2.2 million were left homeless.

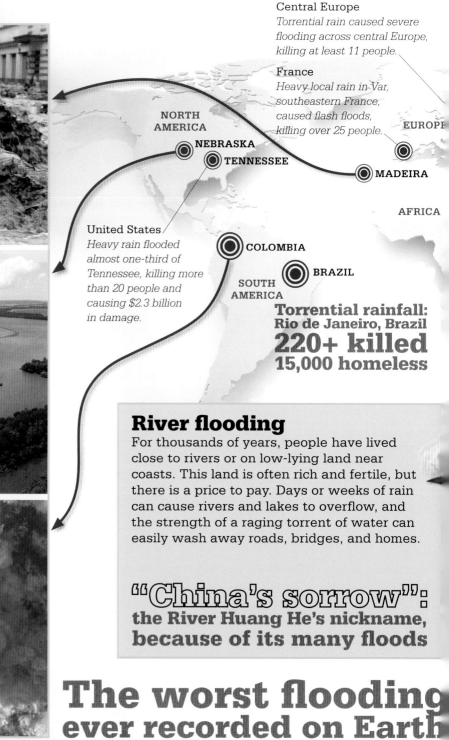

Central Europe
Torrential rain caused severe flooding across central Europe, killing at least 11 people.

France
Heavy local rain in Var, southeastern France, caused flash floods, killing over 25 people.

NORTH AMERICA

NEBRASKA
TENNESSEE

EUROPE

MADEIRA

AFRICA

United States
Heavy rain flooded almost one-third of Tennessee, killing more than 20 people and causing $2.3 billion in damage.

COLOMBIA

BRAZIL

SOUTH AMERICA

Torrential rainfall:
Rio de Janeiro, Brazil
220+ killed
15,000 homeless

River flooding

For thousands of years, people have lived close to rivers or on low-lying land near coasts. This land is often rich and fertile, but there is a price to pay. Days or weeks of rain can cause rivers and lakes to overflow, and the strength of a raging torrent of water can easily wash away roads, bridges, and homes.

"China's sorrow":
the River Huang He's nickname, because of its many floods

The worst flooding ever recorded on Earth

Flood protection

Floods cause so much damage that governments spend time and money on flood prediction and control. Emergency warnings give people time to prepare or evacuate homes. Dams hold back floodwater, releasing it in a controlled way to prevent flooding and loss of life.

Three Gorges Dam
This dam regulates water flow along the River Yangtze, in China, so that lower areas do not flood.

Kazakhstan
Torrential rain and early snowmelt in March caused Kazakhstan's Kyzyl-Agash dam to burst, releasing a torrent of water up to 2 m (6.5 ft) high. Flooding from the reservoir destroyed homes and killed more than 40 people.

ASIA

KAZAKHSTAN

CHINA

THAILAND

UGANDA

Flash floods from late monsoon rains: Thailand
250+ killed

AUSTRALASIA

AUSTRALIA

Record-breaking rainfall:
River Gascoyne
$100 million in
damage
(Australian dollars)

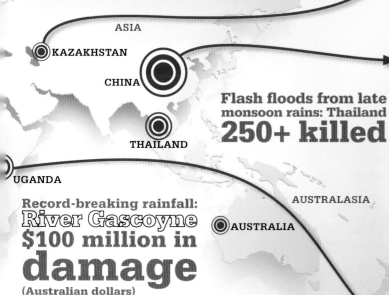

1. Heavy rain falls on waterlogged ground.

2. Runoff pours downhill.

3. River rises rapidly, flooding valley floor.

How rivers flood
If the ground is saturated, rainwater runs across its surface, flooding flat land or filling rivers and lakes until they overflow.

China
Months of prolonged heavy rain caused the flooding of major rivers across most of China's 23 provinces, including Guizhou, in southwestern China. Altogether, around 700 people died across the country, in floods and associated mudslides.

Uganda
Seven hours of continuous heavy rain fell in the mountainous region of Bududa, eastern Uganda, in March. The rain triggered massive mudslides, which buried homes and schools and killed more than 100 people.

3 million+ killed, River Huang He, China, 1931

Marooned
Trapped with his livestock, a man waves at a relief helicopter during the 2010 monsoon floods in Pakistan. Although he is surrounded by water, one of his most urgent needs is clean water for drinking, since the mud-laden floodwaters are polluted and unsafe to drink.

Monsoon floods [Rising water]

In regions with a monsoon climate, such as southern Asia and western Africa, the long dry season is followed by months of torrential rain. The rain is vital for growing crops, but it can spell disaster if rivers overflow their banks, flooding villages and towns.

A human chain
Indian army soldiers rescue two women trapped by rising water after the River Ghaggar burst its banks in 2010.

Eyewitness

NAME: Alamzeb

DATE: August 2010

LOCATION: Pakistan

DETAILS: Alamzeb and his relatives were trapped by monsoon flooding in Nowshera, Pakistan.

❝ We never thought the waters would rise so high. I was away at my aunt's house in the Nowshera Cantonment area. When the waters overflowed the river, I got worried. My relatives said to wait until the tide ebbs, but it kept rising, and soon it was clear that my part of the city had drowned.

My mother died. She was old and diabetic and couldn't climb to the third floor of the house to avoid drowning. My younger brother, who is only 12, tried to drag her up. She was washed away. We haven't found her body. My brother is traumatized. ❞

How monsoons work

During the summer monsoon, or wet season, the wind blows inland, picking up moisture as it crosses the warm waters of the ocean. The moisture falls as rain over the land. The wind changes direction six months later in the dry winter monsoon.

Warm air, moist from evaporated seawater

Hot, humid winds

Warm land, drawing in air from the sea

INDIA

Summer monsoon
In the wet season, the Sun is high in the sky, heating up the land. The moisture-filled monsoon wind blows inland from the sea, bringing heavy rain.

Cool air from mountain regions

Cool, dry winds

INDIA

Winter monsoon
In the dry season, the Sun is lower in the sky. The land cools down, and dry winds blow out to sea.

Rain from humid wind condensed over land

More here

For key to symbols, see page 112

El Niño La Niña **North American monsoon**
West African monsoon
Southwest monsoon
Top End monsoon

Monsoon
by Uma Krishnaswami

Monsoon Summer
by Mitali Perkins

"Monsoon"
(National Geographic Education)
http://education
.nationalgeographic.com/
encyclopedia/monsoon

Find out about monsoons at
http://www.wrh.noaa.gov/
fgz/science/
monsoon.php?who=fgz

Follow monsoons on the website of the Indian Institute of Tropical Meteorology:
http://www.tropmet.res
.in/~kolli/MOL/

evaporate: to change from a liquid to a vapour (gas).

humid: full of water vapour.

monsoon: a wind that changes direction with the seasons. It is derived from the Arabic word *mausim*, meaning "season".

Monsoons in Asia

During the wet summer months, rivers burst their banks and drainage systems often overflow, flooding streets and homes. South and Southeast Asia have the world's most extreme monsoons.

Philippines, 2009
Residents carry inflated inner tubes, in case they are swept off their feet while trying to cross fast-flowing water.

Thailand, 2011
A plane lies stranded at Don Muang airport in Bangkok after the worst monsoon flood in many years.

China, 2011
Apartment buildings in Dazhou are inundated by muddy water, in floods that affected 12 million people.

320 cm: (126 ins) July rainfall in Cherrapunji, India, the wettest place on Earth

Tsunamis [Giant waves]

Most waves are caused when the wind blows across the surface of the sea. Tsunamis are bigger, and much more dangerous. These immense waves are set in motion by earthquakes under the seafloor.

How a tsunami forms

An earthquake below the seabed causes seafloor rocks to shift. This movement pushes up an immense ridge of water. The water spreads out in all directions as waves, which can travel across the open ocean as fast as a passenger plane.

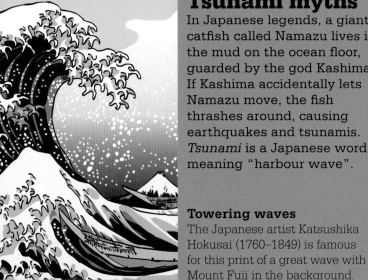

Tsunami myths

In Japanese legends, a giant catfish called Namazu lives in the mud on the ocean floor, guarded by the god Kashima. If Kashima accidentally lets Namazu move, the fish thrashes around, causing earthquakes and tsunamis. *Tsunami* is a Japanese word meaning "harbour wave".

Towering waves

The Japanese artist Katsushika Hokusai (1760–1849) is famous for this print of a great wave with Mount Fuji in the background.

0 sec.

1 Seabed shifts
Two neighbouring plates shift during an earthquake (see page 48). One plate lurches upwards, creating a shortlived ridge of water at the surface.

20 sec.

2 Tsunami begins
Pulled down by gravity, the ridge collapses, triggering a series of waves. The waves race outwards, like ripples from a pebble thrown into a pond.

30 min.

3 Crossing the ocean
The deeper the water, the faster the tsunami travels. In the deep open ocean, the waves can reach speeds of up to 800 kph (500 mph).

Ridge of water
Although not tall, the ridge can be more than 1,000 km (620 miles) long.

DART warning buoy

Ocean waves
In open water, the waves are low in height and spread far apart.

Wave energy
The waves' energy reaches from the surface all the way down to the seabed.

Earthquake epicentre

Earthquake hypocentre or focus

Seabed earthquake detector

TSUNAMI HAZARD ZONE

IN CASE OF EARTHQUAKE, GO
TO HIGH GROUND OR INLAND

520 (1,706 ft) metres:
the world's tallest ever tsunami wave,
Lituya Bay, Alaska, 1958 –
one-and-a-half times as tall as the Eiffel Tower

Tsunami protection

The Indian Ocean tsunami (see pages 74–75) was deadly because no warning system was in place. Since then, a network of quake detectors has been installed. These send signals to floating buoys. Communications satellites pick up the signals and transmit warnings.

NOAA–TSUNAMI

DART warning system
Each DART station consists of an earthquake detector and a floating buoy (above). By sensing seabed earthquakes, DART stations are able to give several hours' warning before a tsunami arrives.

40 min.

4 Approaching land
The waves slow down as they cross shallower coastal waters. They also grow taller – up to 30 times as high as in the open sea.

50 min.

5 Reaching the shore
Before each wave breaks, the sea withdraws up to 1 km (0.5 miles). It then surges forwards, creating a towering wall of water.

Coastal waves
Waves bunch together as the shallow seabed slows them down.

Withdrawing sea

Breaking wave

Spreading inland
When tsunamis reach land, they behave differently from ordinary waves. Instead of breaking on the shore and withdrawing, tsunamis keep on coming. They surge inland, hour after hour, until their energy is used up and the water subsides.

Tsunami timeline

On 26 December 2004, a magnitude 9.1 earthquake struck without warning in the rocks below the Indian Ocean. The earthquake triggered a series of devastating tsunamis.

"I was shocked to see innumerable fishing boats flying on the shoulder of the waves, going back and forth into the sea, as if made of paper"
—P. Ramanamurthy, Andhra Pradesh, India

Spreading out
This map shows how the initial tsunami rippled outwards above the earthquake's epicentre, and how long it took to spread across the Indian Ocean.

+2 HOURS
India hit
In southeast India, the sea receded up to 1 km (0.5 miles) before the waves surged inland. Beach resorts and fishing villages vanished beneath the water, and nearly 10,000 people were killed.

CHENNAI BEACH

+4 HOURS
Maldives swamped
The flat, low-lying Maldives had almost no natural protection against the waves. The capital city was flooded, and around 80 people lost their lives.

+4 hrs +3 hrs

+8 hrs +7 hrs

+2 HOURS 30 MINUTES
Sri Lankan train swept away
Sri Lanka suffered 35,000 casualties, as 6-m (20-ft) waves swamped its shores. On the island's southwest coast, the tsunami hit a crowded passenger train, killing 1,700 people. It was the country's worst ever train disaster.

TWISTED TRAIN TRACKS

+7 HOURS 30 MINUTES
Waves hit Somalia
After crossing 4,500 km (2,800 miles) of open ocean, the first tsunami reached the coast of Somalia in Africa. Even though the waves had become weaker, they still washed away coastal villages, killing more than 200 people and destroying boats and homes. To the south, the Kenyan coast was protected by coral reefs, and only one person drowned.

[Indian Ocean]

7:58 A M
Earthquake began
Pent-up energy was suddenly released in the deep seabed. The earthquake, which shook the ground for ten minutes, jolted trillions of tonnes of water directly above its epicentre, and caused a 1,600-km (1,000-mile) fracture along the seafloor.

+15 MINUTES
First wave
Just fifteen minutes after the ground stopped shaking, the first 10-m (33-ft) wave crashed onto the Banda coast in northern Sumatra, Indonesia. The waves flattened homes and killed around 130,000 people.

SWAMPED LOW-LYING LAND

+2 HOUR **s**
Waves reached Thailand
Within two hours, 5-m (16-ft) waves reached the beaches on the west coast of Thailand. Around 5,000 locals and tourists lost their lives. Some were carried out to sea and drowned. Others were crushed by the force of the water, or by debris carried in the waves.

TSUNAMI HITTING PHUKET BEACH

+1 hr

Wave height
In the open ocean, the tsunamis were only 50 cm (20 ins) high. As they entered shallow coastal waters, they grew until they were 5–10 m (16–33 ft) tall.

10 m — 35 ft
— 30 ft
8 m — 25 ft
6 m — 20 ft
— 15 ft
4 m — 10 ft
2 m — 5 ft

Patong Beach
These photos show the area before (left) and after (right) the tsunami struck.

The invading sea

Japan was hit by disaster in March 2011, when an undersea earthquake triggered a series of tsunamis. Smashing their way over defenses erected against floods, the giant waves surged up to 10 km (6 miles) inland, dragging away millions of tonnes of debris each time they withdrew, and killing more than 19,800 people.

More here
For key to symbols, see page 112

amplitude draw back
rogue wave **tidal wave**
wavelength

Witness to Disaster:
Tsunamis
by Judy and Dennis Fradin

Wave of Destruction:
The Stories of Four
Families and History's
Deadliest Tsunami
by Erich Krauss

"Japan Tsunami"
http://video.national
geographic.com/video/
news/environment-news/
japan-tsunami-2011-vin/

Check out current tsunami
warnings by visiting these
weather sites:
• **Pacific Ocean**
   http://ptwc.weather.gov/
• **Indian Ocean**
   http://ptwc.weather.gov/
   ptwc/index.php?region=3
• **Caribbean Sea**
   http://ptwc.weather.gov/
   ptwc/index.php?region=4

Listen for tsunami alerts
if you are on a coast that
might be affected by
tsunamis. Make sure that
you know the way to the
nearest high ground.

How peo
disa

* How do human activities cause disasters?

* What is global warming?

* Which insect spreads a deadly disease?

Every year, people cause disasters all around the world. These range from wildfires and marine pollution to global warming – potentially the biggest human-caused disaster of all time.

Our troubled world

On today's crowded planet, human activities trigge disasters on a scale never seen before. We damage the natural environment on every continent, making survival harder for other living things. Some human caused disasters strike suddenly, but many others build gradually, over months or years.

Wildfires

In some places, wildfires are part of nature's calendar. Problems arise when people live in areas prone to wildfires, such as this wooded hillside in California. People may spark fires themselves, either by accident or deliberately (see pages 82–83).

Pollution

Pollution is the waste created when we manufacture things, use them, and throw them away. Major pollution disasters may occur by accident. This tanker caught fire in the Gulf of Mexico in 1990, leaking crude oil into the sea.

Deforestation

For thousands of years, people have cut down forests to clear land for farming. Today, it's the turn of tropical forests, such as the Amazon. Deforestation prevents absorption of carbon dioxide, contributing to global warming (see pages 86–89).

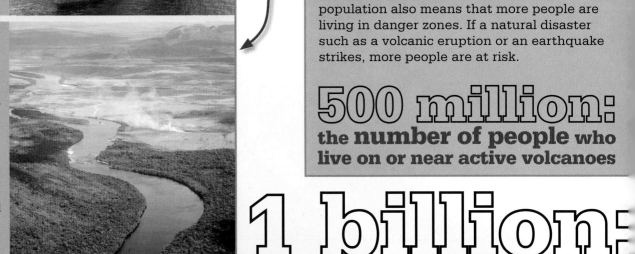

NORTH AMERICA

CALIFORNIA

GULF OF MEXICO

EUROPE
ITALY

Mount Etna

AFRICA

AMAZON RAINFOREST

SOUTH AMERICA

Living in disaster zones

Every year, there seem to be more natural disasters, partly because more of them make the news worldwide. However, our growing population also means that more people are living in danger zones. If a natural disaster such as a volcanic eruption or an earthquake strikes, more people are at risk.

500 million:
the number of people who live on or near active volcanoes

1 billion

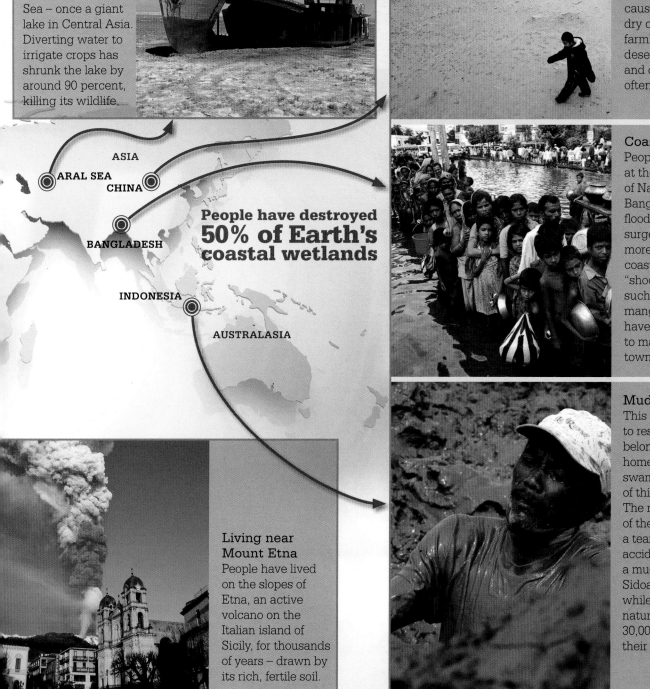

Enviromental disasters
This rusty trawler sits on the dried-up bed of the Aral Sea – once a giant lake in Central Asia. Diverting water to irrigate crops has shrunk the lake by around 90 percent, killing its wildlife.

Desertification
In the Gansu province of China, overfarming has reduced supplies of underground water, causing the soil to dry out and reducing farmland to dusty desert. Desertification and drought can often lead to famine.

Coastal flooding
People line up for aid at the flooded port of Narayanganj, in Bangladesh. Coastal flooding during storm surges has become more common along coasts where natural "shock absorbers", such as wetlands and mangrove forests, have been destroyed to make way for towns and cities.

ASIA

ARAL SEA
CHINA

BANGLADESH

INDONESIA

AUSTRALASIA

People have destroyed 50% of Earth's coastal wetlands

Mud volcanoes
This man is trying to rescue his belongings from his home, which was swamped by streams of thick, toxic mud. The mud oozed out of the ground when a team of engineers accidentally triggered a mud volcano at Sidoarjo, Indonesia, while drilling for natural gas. Around 30,000 people lost their homes.

Living near Mount Etna
People have lived on the slopes of Etna, an active volcano on the Italian island of Sicily, for thousands of years – drawn by its rich, fertile soil.

the number of people
affected worldwide by desertification

Wildfires

[All ablaze]

Raging across grasslands or through forests, wildfires can spread quickly across the countryside, bringing disaster to anyone caught in their paths. They spread fastest in hot weather, when vegetation is dry.

Sparking a wildfire

Many wildfires spark naturally, from a bolt of lightning. Others are caused when fires lit to clear land for farming get out of control. Some start through human carelessness – such as a discarded cigarette butt.

Ignition
This provides the initial source of heat, which sets fuel alight.

The fire triangle
A wildfire needs oxygen and fuel to make it burn, as well as a source of ignition.

O_2

Fuel
Fuels include wood, grass, brush, and peat (soil made of rotted vegetation).

Oxygen
Oxygen reacts with the fuel, releasing large amounts of heat.

How fire spreads

Wildfires spread rapidly if there is a large fuel supply and hot, windy weather fans the flames. Winds usually blow up hills, since warm air rises. So fires rage upwards on sloping ground.

FUEL SUPPLY

WEATHER

TYPE OF LAND

Fanning the flames

Fires are a natural feature of dry forests and scrubland – some plants even depend on the heat to release their seeds. However, the number of fires is steadily on the rise. Three-quarters of all wildfires are started by humans. Each year, there are more than 100,000 wildfires in the United States alone.

Charred seed cone

Surviving the flames
This Australian banksia has adapted to withstand periodic naturally occuring wildfires, only releasing its seeds when scorched.

Eyewitness

NAME: Unknown

DATE: 7 February 2009

LOCATION: Warrandyte, Victoria, Australia

DETAILS: This eyewitness was one of the crew on a North Warrandyte fire engine (Strike Team 1364) battling to put out the Black Saturday wildfires.

❝ We tried to stop the fire [from] jumping a road, but it was impossible due to . . . [100 kph (62 mph) winds and 48°C (118°F) temperatures]. The fire . . . raced through the forest, destroying houses and killing people inside. ❞

Deadly wildfires

Wildfires have caused a number of major disasters over the last 150 years. Most have struck forests, but some have destroyed cities and towns. In the past, when buildings were often made of wood and fire services were limited, hundreds of people sometimes perished in the flames.

1871

United States
On 8 October fire broke out in Chicago, Illinois. During the blaze, 90,000 people lost their homes.

Chicago in flames
Strong winds blew burning embers into the centre of the city, helping the fire spread.

Superscooper
The Canadair CL-215 scoops water from lakes and reservoirs, then drops it on wildfires. It can carry 5,000 litres (1,320 gallons) at a time.

Putting out fires

Firefighters use different techniques to control a blaze. Special planes drop water and fire-retardant chemicals. Smoke jumpers parachute into remote areas near the advancing flames to clear brush, cutting off a fire's fuel supply.

Smoke jumper
One of the very first smoke jumpers prepares to leap from a plane during a blaze in Oregon in 1945.

Emergency escape
Threatened by the flames, a fire engine rushes for safety during Australia's Black Saturday, in February 2009. This fire – in Bunyip State Park – was one of several hundred wildfires that day.

1936
Soviet Union
The Kursha-2 settlement, built to house workers who were chopping down local forests, was destroyed in a wildfire. Around 1,200 people died

1949
France
A wildfire in the Landes forest of southwest France killed over 80 firefighters and destroyed around 50,000 hectares (123,000 acres) of bone-dry trees.

1987
China and the Soviet Union
The Black Dragon Fire, one of the biggest wildfires of recent times, burned 7 million hectares (18 million acres) of forest near the Amur River.

2007
Greece
Fanned by hot winds and encouraged by drought, forest fires blazed in several areas of Greece. The fires killed more than 80 people.

2009
Australia
In Victoria, the Black Saturday bushfires killed 173 people and injured over 400. It was the worst recorded wildfire disaster in the state's history.

Thirsty work

For these Turkana women in northern Kenya, a drought means a lot of extra work. To collect water, they have to climb down a deep well in a dry riverbed, using steps that have been dug by hand. Droughts are natural events, although unlike most disasters, they can last for many years. In places that normally have dry climates (such as northern Kenya), people are used to water shortages. However, prolonged droughts can lead to great hardship. The dry, dusty ground makes it impossible to raise cattle or grow crops, and the result can be famine – one of the biggest disasters of all.

Global warming [Causes]

You can't see it or feel it, but Earth's climate is changing. By burning fossil fuels, we are making our planet warmer – a change that could spell disaster for us and for all living things.

Long-term damage

The Earth is warming because we are pouring greenhouse gases into the atmosphere. These gases include carbon dioxide, or CO_2, which is released when fossil fuels such as coal and oil are burned. Once carbon dioxide is in the atmosphere, it can stay there for over 100 years.

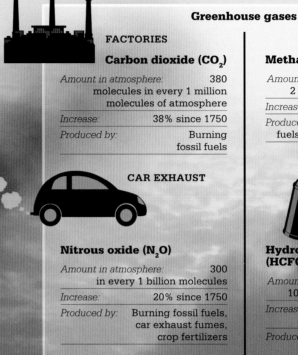

Greenhouse gases

FACTORIES

Carbon dioxide (CO_2)

Amount in atmosphere:	380 molecules in every 1 million molecules of atmosphere
Increase:	38% since 1750
Produced by:	Burning fossil fuels

CATTLE

Methane (CH_4)

Amount in atmosphere:	Less than 2 in every 1 million molecules
Increase:	148% since 1750
Produced by:	Burning fossil fuels, decomposing waste, cattle

CAR EXHAUST

Nitrous oxide (N_2O)

Amount in atmosphere:	300 in every 1 billion molecules
Increase:	20% since 1750
Produced by:	Burning fossil fuels, car exhaust fumes, crop fertilizers

AEROSOLS

Hydrochlorofluorocarbons (HCFCs)

Amount in atmosphere:	Less than 10 in every 1 billion molecules
Increase:	Non-existent before 20th century
Produced by:	Coolants, refrigeration, aerosols

Power stations

Our modern lifestyles demand more energy for our homes and factories. Power stations burn fossil fuels to generate electricity, releasing CO_2.

Greenhouse effect

Earth is kept warm by the greenhouse effect, in which some of the Sun's heat is trapped by greenhouse gases. Without this natural feature of the atmosphere, parts of our planet would freeze. However, the effect is intensified because of the increase of greenhouse gases in the air.

How it works

Greenhouse gases trap heat from the Sun. The more gas there is, the warmer Earth becomes.

1. Sun's energy
Heat from the Sun reaches the Earth's atmosphere. Some is reflected, but most passes through to reach the ground.

2. Heat from Earth
The Earth's surface radiates heat back towards space.

3. Trapped heat
Some of the outgoing heat is trapped by greenhouse gases in the atmosphere.

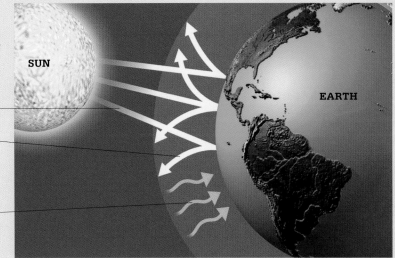

SUN

EARTH

Carbon emissions

Everything we buy or use has a carbon "footprint". This is the amount of carbon dioxide emitted during manufacture, transport, and use. Large industrialized nations emit more carbon than poorer nations do, because they use a lot more energy.

Top ten
The top ten countries in terms of carbon emissions are all in the Northern Hemisphere. China leads, followed by the USA and India.

Carbon footprint
The more things you buy and use, from clothes to electronics, the bigger your carbon footprint becomes.

1 CHINA **8,320** millions of tonnes		**2** UNITED STATES **5,610** millions of tonnes
3 INDIA **1,695** millions of tonnes		**4** RUSSIA **1,633** millions of tonnes
5 JAPAN **1,164** millions of tonnes		**6** GERMANY **793** millions of tonnes
7 SOUTH KOREA **578** millions of tonnes		**8** IRAN **560** millions of tonnes
9 CANADA **548** millions of tonnes		**10** UNITED KINGDOM **532** millions of tonnes

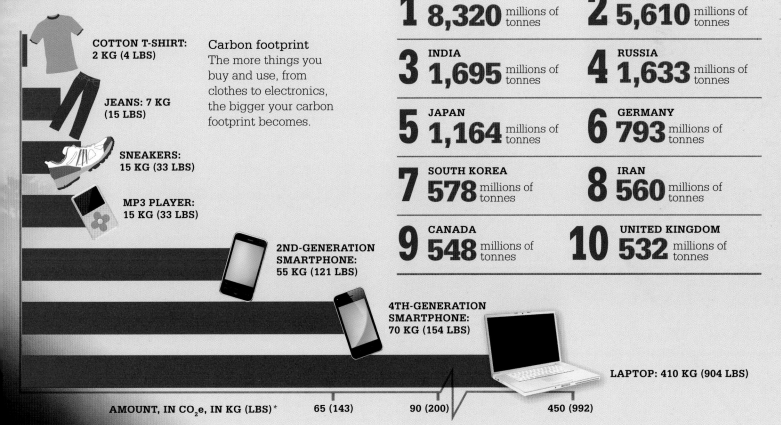

COTTON T-SHIRT: 2 KG (4 LBS)

JEANS: 7 KG (15 LBS)

SNEAKERS: 15 KG (33 LBS)

MP3 PLAYER: 15 KG (33 LBS)

2ND-GENERATION SMARTPHONE: 55 KG (121 LBS)

4TH-GENERATION SMARTPHONE: 70 KG (154 LBS)

LAPTOP: 410 KG (904 LBS)

AMOUNT, IN CO_2e, IN KG (LBS)*   65 (143)   90 (200)   450 (992)

*CO_2e stands for CO_2 equivalent – the total emission of all greenhouse gases, expressed as the equivalent amount of CO_2

Getting warmer [Effects]

Imagine how you would feel if your home disappeared beneath the ocean waves. That's the prospect facing some island nations as the world continues to warm. Sea level rise is just one of the effects of global warming. Other changes are also underway – and the warmer it gets, the more disastrous they will be.

Disappearing world

Even in the next few decades, sea level rise may make low-lying islands across the world uninhabitable. Their land area will shrink, storm damage will increase, and there will be no freshwater.

Islands in danger

Micronesia, in the Pacific Ocean, has thousands of low-lying island nations. Kiribati, pictured, has over 30 islands, all of them less than 2 m (6.5 ft) above the high-tide mark.

Eyewitness

NAME: James Bing
DATE: 2012
LOCATION: Marshall Islands, Micronesia
DETAILS: James Bing, a Marshall Islander, remembers his home.

❝ During my 20 years of living in the Marshall Islands I have noticed climate change happening. The islands are getting smaller. . . . The land and soil is being washed away slowly. . . . Every year during the king tide season, I remember it not being a big deal. . . . Now it's different – you can see the water flooding the streets and homes. ❞

World effects

Scientists have been studying some of the disastrous effects of global warming since the 1980s, from the impact on a small reef ecosystem to that on a whole continent. While some people doubt that global warming is taking place or that it is caused by humans, most scientists believe that the evidence is now all around us.

Melting glaciers

Mountain glaciers and ice caps are melting and retreating worldwide. Their meltwater ends up in the oceans, contributing to sea level rise.

Dying reefs

Corals cannot survive in water that is too warm or contains too much dissolved CO_2. In the tropics, reefs are "bleaching" and dying off.

Extinction

Animals are at risk from climate change. Many species of some amphibians, for example, have already become extinct because of global warming and disease.

If Earth gets hotter

If Earth's average temperature continues to rise, disasters that are already occurring will intensify. Just a few degrees hotter, and we could be in danger of a catastrophe.

4–5°C (7.2–9.0°F) increase
- Devastating wildfires and storms;
- Acidification of seawater from dissolved CO_2 speeds the extinction of marine life;
- Widespread extinction of animals and plants.

3–4°C (5.4–7.2°F) increase
- Large areas of forest are destroyed by wildfires;
- Low-lying coasts have to be evacuated;
- Collapse of fish populations;
- Increased risk of illness as disease-carrying insects, such as mosquitoes, spread;
- Crop production fails in many regions.

2–3°C (3.6–5.4°F) increase
- Sea level rise speeds up as more glaciers melt;
- Widespread death of coral reefs;
- Changing ocean currents begin to affect the global climate;
- Millions are displaced by coastal flooding.

1–2°C (1.8–3.6°F) increase
- Up to 30 percent of species are at increasing risk of extinction;
- Most corals bleached; reefs begin to die;
- Millions of people suffer water shortages;
- Crop production fails in some regions;
- Devastating floods and storms.

0–1°C (0–1.8°F) increase
- Sea level rises at a rate of about 4 mm (0.16 ins) a year;
- Risk of wildfires, floods, and storms;
- Frequent droughts in midlatitudes;
- More rainfall in the tropics.

Temperature chart
The projections in this chart are from the United Nations' Intergovernmental Panel on Climate Change (IPCC).

Carbon emissions

How much our planet will warm depends on many things, including whether countries cut down on carbon emissions, and how quickly they manage to do so.

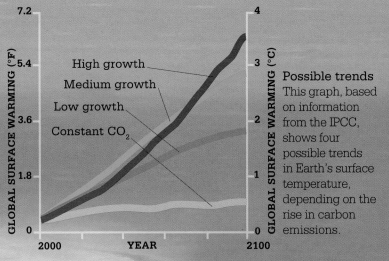

Possible trends This graph, based on information from the IPCC, shows four possible trends in Earth's surface temperature, depending on the rise in carbon emissions.

Coastline flooding

If Earth's average sea level continues to rise, more coastlines will be flooded. A rise of up to 1 m (3.3 ft) – predicted by the year 2100 – could displace millions.

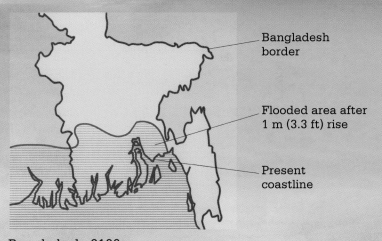

Bangladesh border

Flooded area after 1 m (3.3 ft) rise

Present coastline

Bangladesh, 2100
Low-lying Bangladesh in Southeast Asia, one of the world's poorest nations, will be badly affected by sea level rise.

Bangladesh, 2100:
17 million people affected, 20% of the country underwater

Tackling global warming

Global warming cannot be stopped, because it is already happening. But we can prevent a runaway disaster by changing how we live – from the way that we get energy to the things that we buy and use.

Reducing greenhouse gases

Around the world, countries have set themselves goals for reducing CO_2 emissions. Five main goals are shown on these two pages. Two of them – recycling household waste and using renewable energy sources – are things that everyone can do.

Wind turbines

A typical wind turbine can generate 5 million kilowatt-hours (kWh) of electricity a year – that's enough to power 1,000 homes.

1
Renewable energy
Nuclear power is a way of producing electricity without emitting carbon. However, it is controversial because of the risk of nuclear disaster.

2
Reforestation
Planting forests helps remove CO_2 from the atmosphere, because trees use and store carbon as they grow. It stays locked inside while the trees are alive.

Car carbon emissions:*

Gas-powered
24.5 kg CO_2 per 100 km
(87 lbs per 100 miles)

Hybrid electric
16 kg CO_2 per 100 km
(57 lbs per 100 miles)

All-electric
15 kg CO_2 per 100 km
(54 lbs per 100 miles)

* Includes all emissions related to fuel production, processing, distribution, and use

3
Smart meters
Electronic meters monitor and adjust energy use in factories, offices, and home to keep it at a minimum.

[Going green]

Carbon capture and storage

Some countries are looking into emergency measures that can help limit our CO_2 output. One idea involves capturing and storing carbon before it escapes into the air. The carbon would be stored inside rocks below the seabed.

How it works
CO_2 is pumped underground and stored, instead of being released into the atmosphere.

1. Capture
CO_2 is captured at power stations where fossil fuels are burned.

2. Collection
Compressed CO_2 is pumped to natural gas-drilling rigs at sea.

3. Burial
The gas is pumped into tiny holes in sandstone that once held natural gas.

4. Storage
The CO_2 can remain trapped inside for millions of years.

4 Farming
Biofuel crops such as maize or sugarcane can be used to power vehicles. They can take the place of fuels such as gas and diesel.

5 Energy from waste
Non-recyclable waste can be burned and used to generate electricity. This helps to reduce fossil fuel consumption and also reduces the amount of dumped waste.

Recycling

Recycling doesn't just get rid of rubbish – it also reduces your carbon footprint. Making things from recycled materials takes much less energy than making them from raw materials. The percentage amounts of energy saved are shown below.

Aluminium can 95%

Paper 40%

Plastic water bottle 30%

More here

For key to symbols, see page 112

carbon footprint
Kyoto Protocol **hydropower**
renewable energy
carbon neutrality **IPCC**
geothermal energy

The Carbon Diaries 2015
by Saci Lloyd

Under the Weather: Stories about Climate Change
edited by Tony Bradman

Visit the **Centre for Alternative Techology**, at Machynlleth, Powys. Find out about alternative energy and eco-friendly housing at this centre in rural Wales.

Switch off electrical appliances when they are not being used.

Put on an extra layer of clothing instead of turning up the heat.

Reduce your household waste by sorting paper, glass, and plastic so that they can be recycled.

Make a compost bin to recycle food waste.

Walk or ride your bike to meet your friends instead of going by car.

Overburdened Earth

Seen from space at night, Earth is a sparkling web of light that shows the spread of people across its surface, especially densely populated cities. With 250 babies born each minute, our world's population is growing by nearly 74 million per year. Every one of us uses energy, which places increasing pressure on Earth's dwindling natural resources and contributes to global warming (see pages 86–87).

The United Nations called 31 October 2011

7 Bill

on Day: the day the world's **population** reached 7 billion

Pandemics [Killer diseases]

Global outbreaks of infectious diseases have brought disaster to humankind. Some pandemics, such as influenza (flu) and cholera, still break out across the world, affecting millions each year.

1500s
Measles

In many parts of the world, measles is endemic, or always present, and people develop a resistance to it. However, it was unknown in the Americas before the Europeans arrived. The Europeans carried measles, as well as smallpox and mumps, with them. This triggered disastrous epidemics that claimed over 10 million lives in the Inca and Aztec empires.

AZTEC DRAWING OF VICTIM

800 BCE
Early plagues

PLAGUE AMULET

Dating from 800–612 BCE , this Assyrian amulet, or lucky charm, was meant to protect its owner from the plague. *Plague* originally meant any infectious disease that killed large numbers of people.

165–180 CE
The Antonine Plague was either smallpox or measles. It killed 2,000 people a day in the city of Rome, with a final death toll of 5 million.

1096
Typhus emerged in Europe during the Crusades. Spread by lice, it is sometimes called camp fever.

CRUSADER KNIGHT

1492
Deadly diseases, such as smallpox and measles, were introduced into the Americas by Europeans.

• 800 BCE   •1100   • 1300   • 1500

---

430 BCE
The Plague of Athens was probably an outbreak of typhoid fever, which raged for over four years in ancient Greece.

541–750 CE
The Plague of Justinian was the first recorded outbreak of bubonic plague. It killed 25 million people in Europe before finally fading away.

1580
The first influenza pandemic was recorded in Europe. It had spread from Asia, via Africa.

FLEA-CARRYING BLACK RAT

50% of Europe's population **was killed by plague between 1346 and 1355**

MID -1300 S
The Black Death

The Black Death was an outbreak of bubonic plague, which came to Europe in October 1346, probably from eastern Asia. Spread by fleas from rats and by physical contact, it often caused painful swellings, called buboes, on the body, giving the disease its name. There was no known treatment. Infected families were often shut inside their homes, left to their fates.

ILLUSTRATION OF THE BLACK DEATH FROM THE TOGGENBURG BIBLE (1411)

PAINTING OF DEATH BRINGING CHOLERA

1600s
Typhus

This killer disease thrives in crowded, insanitary conditions – the kind found in prisons and in soldiers' camps during wartime. In Europe, the disease caused millions of deaths between the 17th and 20th centuries. The first vaccine to protect against typhus was developed in 1937.

Typhus **killed** a third of the people it infected in the 1600s

DOCTOR WEARING A BIRD MASK THOUGHT TO PROTECT AGAINST PLAGUE

1816
Cholera

Cholera is easily spread by contaminated water and food. The first pandemic swept through southern Asia in 1816, causing hundreds of thousands of deaths. Six more pandemics followed. The first vaccine for the disease was developed in the late 19th century.

1918
Spanish flu

This pandemic killed up to 50 million people worldwide in 1918–1919, more than all of the deaths caused by World War I. The first vaccine against flu was developed in 1945.

Spanish flu killed **50 million** (and infected 25% of the world's population)

VICTIMS IN A TEMPORARY HOSPITAL

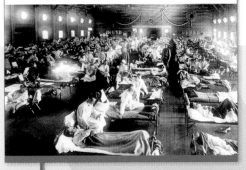

1793
Yellow fever struck Philadelphia, Pennsylvania, USA, killing about 10 percent of the city's population.

1897
The first vaccine against bubonic plague was developed.

•1700

•1900

1665
The Great Plague of London, an outbreak of bubonic plague, killed at least 100,000 people, emptying the city's streets.

1956–58
Avian flu broke out in China, triggering a global pandemic and killing up to 4 million worldwide.

1963
The first vaccine for measles was developed.

Present
The world's biggest killer diseases are respiratory infections, like the flu.

1764
Smallpox

In 1764, the English doctor Edward Jenner carried out a successful vaccination against smallpox – one of the world's deadliest diseases. For centuries, smallpox killed or disfigured millions every year. In 1958, a worldwide vaccination programme was launched, and the last case of smallpox was recorded in 1977.

1981
HIV/AIDS

First identified in 1981 in the United States, the human immunodeficiency virus (HIV) has since spread worldwide. AIDS, the disease caused by the virus, has already killed more than 30 million people. The worst-affected country is South Africa, where it claims over 300,000 lives a year.

MAGNIFICATION OF AIDS VIRUS PARTICLES BUDDING ON A HUMAN LYMPH CELL

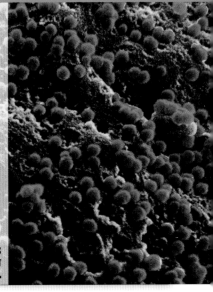

Tiny killer
Magnified over 100 times, a female *Anopheles* mosquito gets ready for a meal of human blood. The amount it drinks is tiny, but as it feeds it can introduce parasites that cause malaria. The mosquito can then spread the disease when it bites its next victims.

Malaria

Malaria is a natural disaster – and a human one. For thousands of years, it has been one of the most deadly infectious diseases. Parasites transmitted by mosquitoes multiply in a person's liver and blood. This causes severe headaches, liver damage, and potentially fatal fevers. Today, more than 90 percent of malaria-related deaths occur in Africa, where people and carrier mosquitoes often mix. Worldwide, one child dies every minute from malaria.

Spread of malaria
Malarial mosquitoes thrive in warm tropical regions. This map shows the areas affected by malaria in 2010. About 665,000 people died from the disease that year.

Preventing malaria

Mosquitoes breed in stagnant water, so draining ponds and ditches makes it harder for them to survive. Using nets helps prevent bites, because the insects cannot fly through the fine mesh. If the nets are treated with insecticide, the mosquitoes die

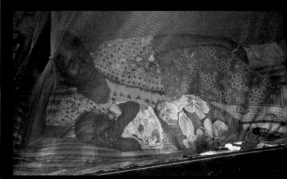

Expensive nets
Drugs, insecticides, and even nets are too expensive for many in regions where malaria is endemic. Money is desperately needed for researching new drugs and vaccines.

The thr
Spa

* When will the Sun destroy our planet?

* How do solar storms affect our daily lives?

* What is an asteroid strike?

eat from ace

Asteroid strike

About 65 million years ago, a huge asteroid plunged through the atmosphere and smashed into Earth. The dinosaurs and many other animals were wiped out as fires raged and clouds of debris filled the air. It was a global disaster – and it could happen again.

Target Earth

Ever since Earth formed, it has been bombarded by rocks from space. Meteorites, or small rocks, fall to Earth without causing any damage. Asteroids are much bigger and much more dangerous. The one that killed off the dinosaurs was at least 10 km (6 miles) wide and weighed over 1 trillion tonnes.

Craters on the Moon

On Earth, impact craters from asteroids are worn away until few traces remain. But the Moon has no weather, so its craters are easy to see – clear evidence of the many impacts the Moon has experienced since it formed over 4 billion years ago.

Fatal impact

Travelling at 50 times the speed of sound, a 1-trillion-tonne asteroid would have unimaginable destructive power. It could gouge out an impact crater 180 km (110 miles) wide, then instantly vaporize, blocking out light from the Sun. In the months of darkness that would follow, three-quarters of the world's plants would die.

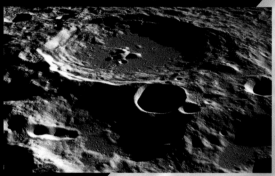

Large and small
Many of the Moon's craters are smaller than a pinhead. The largest are over 300 km (185 miles) wide.

Near-Earth objects

NASA constantly monitors near-Earth objects (NEOs) that speed past Earth on their orbits around the Sun. Most are not dangerous, but some come closer to Earth than our Moon does. If one was tugged off course by Earth's gravity, it could hit our planet, with devastating results.

Local devastation		Regional devastation		Extinction event	
NEO's size:	25 m (82 ft) in diameter – the size of a house	*NEO's size:*	50 m (164 ft) in diameter – as tall as a 15-storey office building	*NEO's size:*	1.5 km (1 mile) in diameter – the length of 15 football fields
Speed:	50,000 kph (31,000 mph)	*Speed:*	50,000 kph (31,000 mph)	*Speed:*	50,000 kph (31,000 mph)
Could destroy:	An area up to 2.5 km (1.5 miles) wide	*Could destroy:*	A major city	*Could destroy:*	Most of life on Earth

Tunguska fireball

In 1908, a mysterious fireball destroyed a huge expanse of forest around Tunguska, a remote village in central Siberia, Russia. The explosion was probably caused by a meteoroid or comet breaking up high above the ground.

Flattened forest
Signs of the Tunguska event were still visible nearly 20 years later, although the explosion left no crater.

Eyewitness

NAME: Unknown

DATE: 30 June 1908

LOCATION: 30 km (19 miles) from the Tunguska River, in Russia

DETAILS: Interviewed by a scientific expedition, a reindeer herder described what he saw and heard during the Tunguska event.

❝ The ground shook and incredibly prolonged roaring was heard. Everything round about was shrouded in smoke and fog from burning, falling trees. Eventually the noise died away and the wind dropped, but the forest went on burning. **❞**

More here

For key to symbols, see page 112

Near-Earth object
asteroid belt **Ceres**
radiant (meteor shower)
shooting stars

Killer Rocks from Outer Space: Asteroids, Comets, and Meteorites
by Steven N. Koppes

"Doomsday Asteroid"
http://www.nasa.gov/
topics/universe/features/
asteroid-collision_prt.htm

See shooting stars fall to Earth during a meteor shower. There's no need for binoculars – just find somewhere away from artificial light. Peak times:
• Perseids: 13 August
• Leonids: 17 November
• Geminids: 14 December

Keep up-to-date with near-Earth objects at
http://neo.jpl.nasa.gov/

meteor: the visible trace of a meteoroid passing through the atmosphere.

meteorite: a meteoroid that reaches Earth's surface instead of burning up in the atmosphere.

meteoroid: a small particle of debris or rock travelling through space.

Asteroids are not the only hazard that threatens us from space. The Sun – our nearest star – seethes with energy, which sometimes erupts in colossal solar storms. An extra-large storm can knock out electric systems on Earth, bringing normal life to a halt.

Swirling surface
Telescopes on Earth must be shielded by special filters to observe solar storms. This view shows a single prominence, big enough to swallow 1,000 Earths.

The solar maximum
The Sun has a strong magnetic field that builds up to a stormy maximum every 9–14 years, with maximums in 2000 and 2013. During a solar maximum, planet-size sunspots track across the surface of the Sun, while loop-shaped prominences arch into space. Energy and matter are ejected in solar flares.

A future solar storm could

In the line of fire
As energy and matter stream outwards from the Sun, they create huge disturbances in space, affecting all of the planets that they pass. Earth is one of the inner planets, so it feels the full impact. Farther out in the solar system, the effect of solar storms dwindles. When the Sun is quiet, flares occur less than once a week, but at the height of a storm, they can occur every day. Giant flares can be longer than the distance between Earth and the Moon.

Sun's magnetic field

Solar flare
A flare erupts from an area of intense magnetic activity.

CME
A coronal mass ejection (CME) is produced as the flare streams into space.

Sunspots
Pairs of sunspots are often connected by curved solar prominences.

How a solar flare works
As a solar flare bursts through the corona, or the outer layer of the Sun's atmosphere, it often forces out clouds of charged particles. This coronal mass ejection (CME) produces solar energetic particles (SEPs). They can cause disturbances in Earth's magnetic field.

The 1859 solar storm

In August 1859, the largest solar storm ever reported was seen on the Sun's surface. It featured giant sunspots and solar flares. Within hours, Earth's magnetic field was disrupted, and the first effects were felt around the world. Telegraph systems failed, and brilliantly coloured auroras shimmered in the skies as far south as Cuba, Hawaii, and Rome in Italy.

Auroras

Auroras are lights that appear in the sky, usually at high latitudes near Earth's magnetic poles. They are created when charged particles from the Sun collide with atoms high up in Earth's atmosphere. Auroras are brightest during solar storms, when there is increased activity on the Sun's surface.

Northern lights

Sometimes called the northern lights, auroras are usually bluish-green and appear to hang in the sky like curtains.

Out of action

During the storm, sparks cascaded from telegraph equipment, blocking communications around the globe.

Wires on fire

Bursts of current set overhead telegraph wires on fire.

knock out electricity worldwide

SEPs
A CME produces solar energetic particles (SEPs).

Earth

Effects on Earth

A repeat of the 1859 solar storm would have serious effects on Earth, since we now rely so heavily on electric power. Power grids could be disrupted, as well as anything electronic, including global positioning systems (GPS) and vital hospital equipment.

SEPs
SEPs stream through space in straight lines.

Shock wave
A mass of SEPs produces a shockwave.

Wave at Earth
A wave of SEPs causes geomagnetic storms on Earth.

Shaped by the Sun
Earth's magnetic field forms a "tail" as SEPs stream past.

A world without the Internet
A solar storm could affect the Internet by disabling electronics and cutting off power.

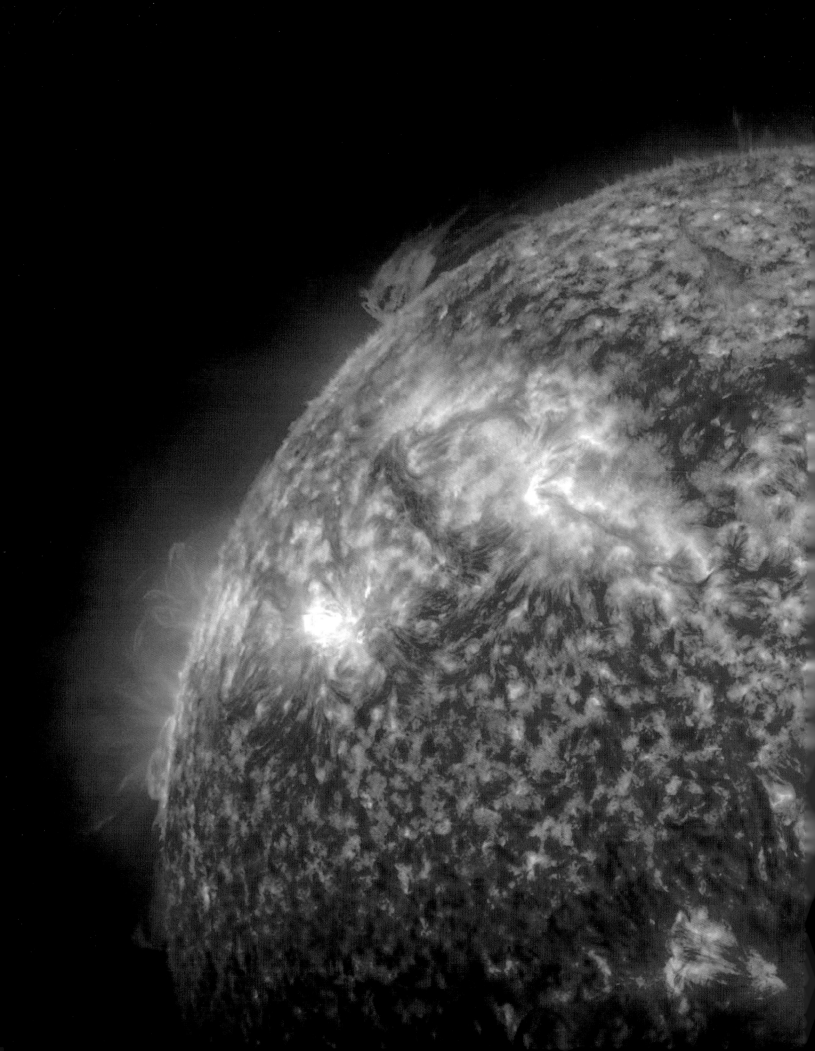

The final disaster

Almost all life on Earth depends on heat and light from the Sun. However, like all stars, the Sun will change as it ages. In about 1 billion years, as it starts to run out of fuel, it will begin to swell, until it eventually engulfs our planet and wipes out all traces of past life.

aa lava
Thick, sticky lava that has a rough surface when it solidifies.

acidification
A chemical reaction that makes a substance acidic. Seawater acidifies when it dissolves carbon dioxide from the air.

aftershock
A small earthquake that happens after a bigger quake. Aftershocks are dangerous because they can cause already damaged buildings to collapse.

asteroid
A large piece of rock or a miniature planet that orbits (travels around) the Sun.

biofuel
A fuel made from plants. Biofuel crops include corn, sugarcane, and sunflowers, as well as many other plants that produce oils rich in energy.

carbon dioxide
A colourless gas found in the atmosphere, absorbed by plants when they grow. It plays an important role in the greenhouse effect.

carbon footprint
The amount of carbon-containing gas emitted by things that we use (such as a lights, computers, or cars) and actions that we take (such as manufacturing goods).

cinder cone
A volcano with a wide, steep crater composed of small pieces of lava.

comet
A piece of rock and ice orbiting the Sun. Unlike asteroids, comets often have long tails of dust and gas.

condensation funnel
In a tornado, a funnel formed by droplets of water.

conduit
A vertical tunnel in a volcano that allows magma to flow upwards into a volcano's vent.

convergent boundary
A type of boundary in Earth's crust where neighbouring plates collide head-on.

coral bleaching
An effect on corals that results when the sea gets too warm. The corals turn white because they expel the colourful algae that normally live inside them.

core
The innermost region of Earth, composed mainly of iron. This creates Earth's magnetic field.

cornice
An overhanging slab of snow on top of a mountain ridge. A cornice comes to a sharp edge that points away from the wind.

corona
The outermost layer of the Sun, which stretches far into space. The corona is composed of charged particles and has a temperature of over 1,000,000°C (1,800,000°F).

crust
The rocky outer layer of Earth, whether under the sea or exposed as dry land.

DART
An automated tsunami warning system that uses surface buoys and seismometers on the seabed. The seismometers detect seabed earthquakes, and the buoys pass the signals to satellites. *DART* stands for *Deep-Ocean Assessment and Reporting of Tsunamis.*

deforestation
Destruction of forests, for their timber or to clear land for farms.

divergent boundary
A type of boundary in Earth's crust at which neighbouring plates pull apart.

doldrums
At sea, a zone of light winds that stretches around the Equator.

endemic
Present in a given place or region.

epicentre
The point on Earth's surface directly above the hypocentre, where an earthquake starts.

evaporate
To change from a liquid to a vapour (gas).

extinction
The permanent disappearance of a species of animal or plant after the last of the species has died out.

eye
In a hurricane, the clear, calm zone at the centre of the storm.

fault
A crack in Earth's crust where blocks of rock slip past one another. Faults vary hugely in size – some are small, but others are thousands of kilometres long.

flash flood
A sudden flood caused by a storm.

fossil fuel
A fuel that is formed from the ancient remains of living things. Fossil fuels include coal, oil, and natural gas. They contain high levels of carbon, and they release carbon dioxide when they are burned.

geologist
A scientist who studies Earth.

global warming
A change in Earth's climate that causes the planet to warm up. Global warming has happened many times in the past and is happening now.

greenhouse effect
The trapping of heat by gases in a planet's atmosphere. The greenhouse effect keeps Earth warm by absorbing energy that would otherwise escape into space.

greenhouse gas
Any gas in the atmosphere that plays a part in the greenhouse effect. The most important greenhouse gases are carbon dioxide and water vapour.

humid
Full of water vapour.

In the decade 2001–2010, 65% of all people killed in natural disasters lived in the Asia-Pacific region

Glossary

A lightning bolt can reach 30,000°C (54,000°F) – that's five times hotter than the surface of the Sun

hypocentre
The site below the ground where an earthquake starts.

hypothermia
A dangerous drop in body temperature, which can lead to disorientation and even death.

inundate
To completely cover with water.

IPCC
An international group of scientists who study climate change and its future effects. The IPCC was established in 1988 and brings together research from more than 100 countries. *IPCC* stands for *Intergovernmental Panel on Climate Change*.

lahar
A flow of mud or debris, usually triggered by a volcanic eruption.

lava
Magma, or molten rock, that has erupted onto Earth's surface.

lava field
A plain of solidified lava, left behind after volcanic eruptions. Some lava plains can cover hundreds of square kilometres.

magma
Hot, molten rock in Earth's mantle, below the crust. Magma reaches the surface through volcanoes and volcanic vents.

mantle
The layer of Earth between the crust and the core.

meteor
The visible trace of a meteoroid passing through the atmosphere. Meteors are sometimes called shooting stars.

meteorite
A meteoroid that reaches Earth's surface instead of burning up in the atmosphere.

meteoroid
A small particle of debris or rock travelling through space.

meteorologist
A scientist who studies weather and climate.

mid-ocean ridge
A submerged mountain range in the middle of an ocean, where volcanic activity slowly forms new seabed.

monsoon
A wind that changes direction with the seasons. It is derived from the Arabic word *mausim*, meaning "season".

monsoon climate
A tropical climate that has two different seasons – one wet and one dry. The monsoon, or wet season, brings heavy rain.

mudslide
A river of waterlogged mud that rushes downhill in a torrent. Mudslides often occur on slopes after prolonged heavy rain.

normal fault
A crack in Earth's crust at which two neighbouring plates slowly diverge, or pull apart.

pahoehoe lava
Lava that flows easily and that has a glassy skin when it cools.

pandemic
An outbreak of disease that infects many people at the same time.

parasite
An organism that lives inside or on another living thing, using it for food. Small animals can be parasites, as can tiny micro-organisms that cannot be seen with the naked eye.

plate
One of the huge pieces of rock that make up Earth's crust, or outer layer. Plates are slowly moving, usually by 2.5–4 cm (1–1.5 ins) each year.

plug
The hard tower of solid lava that is sometimes left when the rest of a volcano is eroded, or worn away, by the wind and rain.

pollution
Anything that contaminates the natural world and harms living things. Pollutants include gases that escape into the air, and chemicals that find their way into water and soil.

pumice
A light volcanic rock formed from frothy lava. Some kinds of pumice are so lightweight that they can float.

reforestation
Replanting of forests that have been cut down. Reforestation helps counteract global warming, because trees absorb carbon dioxide from the air.

renewable energy
Energy from natural sources that are continuously renewed. It includes energy from the Sun, wind, and moving water, as well as geothermal energy from the ground.

Sahel
A region of Africa, south of the Sahara desert, where rain is scarce and unpredictable. The Sahel stretches from the coast of western Africa to the Red Sea.

saturate
To completely soak with water, so that no more can be absorbed.

seismologist
A geologist who studies earthquakes, their causes, and their effects.

seismometer
An instrument that records vibrations produced by earthquakes. By using seismometers at different locations around the world, scientists can pinpoint an earthquake's epicentre.

shield volcano
A volcano that is shaped like a huge, gently sloping dome. Shield volcanoes are formed from runny lava that spreads easily when it erupts.

During the last 10,000 years, there have been 1,500 active volcanoes on Earth

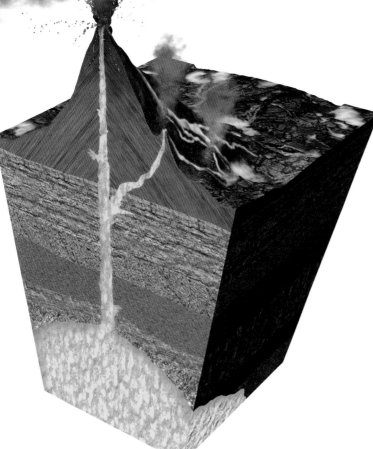

STRATOVOLCANO

stratovolcano
A volcano that is built up from many layers of lava and ash.

strike-slip fault
A crack in the Earth's crust at which two neighbouring plates slide horizontally past each other.

sunspot
A relatively cool patch on the surface of the Sun that appears dark in comparison to its bright surroundings. Sunspots are areas of intense activity on the Sun's surface, caused by the Sun's magnetic field.

supercell
A rotating thunderstorm that can produce tornadoes.

thrust fault
A crack in Earth's crust at which two neighbouring plates converge, or come together. As the plates collide, one is thrust below the other.

Tornado Alley
An area in the US Midwest, stretching from Texas to Nebraska and Iowa, that experiences more tornadoes than any other area in the world.

transform boundary
A type of boundary in Earth's crust at which neighbouring plates slide past one another.

tremor
A shaking or vibrating movement of the earth.

tropical cyclone
A powerful tropical storm that often forms over the sea.

Tropical cyclones include hurricanes, which form over the Atlantic Ocean from May to November, and typhoons, which form over the northwest Pacific Ocean from June to November.

tropical depression
A low-pressure weather system with heavy rain and clouds. Tropical depressions have maximum wind speeds of 63 kph (39 mph).

tropical storm
A storm that starts in the tropics. Tropical storms have maximum wind speeds of 119 kph (74 mph).

tropics
The region between the Tropic of Cancer (23.5 degrees north of the Equator) and the Tropic of Capricorn (23.5 degrees south of the Equator). A tropical climate has high temperatures and heavy rain for at least part of the year.

tuned mass damper
A heavy weight mounted in skyscrapers and other buildings to protect them during an earthquake.

twister
In the USA, a term often used to mean a tornado.

vent
In a volcano, an opening that lets magma escape to the surface of the Earth.

volcanologist
A geologist who studies volcanoes, including how they are formed and how they erupt.

soil creep
The slow downhill movement of soil. Creep often happens in wet conditions, or when soil freezes and then thaws.

solar flare
A sudden eruption of hydrogen gas in the Sun's atmosphere, caused by changes in the Sun's magnetic field.

solar maximum
A peak in the buildup of the Sun's magnetic storms, which occurs every 9–14 years.

solar prominence
A huge, loop-shaped band of glowing gas that stretches outwards from the surface of the Sun.

storm surge
A rise in sea level caused when a hurricane or a typhoon drifts over land.

Index

PHOTOGRAPHY

1: Associated Press; 2–3: AFP/Getty Images; 4–5 (background): NASA; 6: Associated Press; 7l: NASA/Photo Researchers, Inc.; 7cl: iStockphoto; 7cr: Mainichi Newspaper/AFLO/Nippon News/Corbis; 7r: David A. Hardy/AstroArt; 8–9: iStockphoto; 10–11: Mitchell Krog/mitchellkrog.com; 12l: Mike Hollingshead/Photo Researchers, Inc.; 12c: Mitchell Krog/Living Canvas Photography; 12r: Jim Reed/Photo Researchers, Inc.; 14t: public domain; 14c, 14b: Associated Press; 14–15 (maps): Ermek/Shutterstock; 15tl, 15tr, 15c, 15bl, 15br: Associated Press; 16–17 (background): Maksim Shmeljov/Shutterstock; 16–17 (globe): NASA; 16tr: Zhabska Tetyana/Shutterstock; 17bl, 17bcl, 17bcr, 17br: Associated Press; 18, 19tc: Jim Reed/Photo Researchers, Inc.; 19tr: Joshua Wurman, Center for Severe Weather Research; 19cl: NASA; 19cm: Jim Reed/Photo Researchers, Inc.; 19cr: Tad Denson/Shutterstock; 19b: Nick Cobbing/Alamy; 20–21 (background), 20–21c: Mike Hollingshead/Photo Researchers, Inc.; 20–21b: Ryan McGinnis; 21tc, 21tr: Jim Reed/Photo Researchers, Inc.; 22–23, 23br: Ryan McGinnis; 24 (person, cow, train, dog, bus, mattress, fish, car): iStockphoto; 26tl: Jim Reed/Photo Researchers, Inc.; 26–27b: NASA/Photo Researchers, Inc.; 28tc: NOAA; 28tr: Jim Reed/Photo Researchers, Inc.; 28bl: NOAA; 28br: iStockphoto; 29tl: Associated Press; 29tc: Caitlin Mirra/Shutterstock; 29tr: Jason Reed/Reuters/Corbis; 29bl: Digital Globe, Eurimage/Photo Researchers, Inc.; 29br: Katrina's Kids Project; 30–31: Associated Press; 32t: NASA; 32ct, 32cb: iStockphoto; 32bl: Abestrobi; 32br: Associated Press; 32–33: Mitchell Krog; 34–35: Associated Press; 34br: NOAA; 35br: Harper/Shutterstock; 36blt: public domain; 36blb: iStockphoto; 36bc: Nolispanmo; 36br: iStockphoto; 37: Alaska Stock/Alamy; 38–39: Mike Hollingshead/Photo Researchers, Inc.; 40l: Bruce Omori/epa/Corbis; 40c: Associated Press; 40r: Romeo Ranoco/X00226/Reuters/Corbis; 42–43: Inayat Ali (Shimshal); 42 (landslide illustrations): Gary Hincks/Photo Researchers, Inc.; 43tr, 43cr, 43br: Associated Press; 45tl, 45tcl: iStockphoto; 45tcr: Associated Press; 45tr: iStockphoto; 45b: Claus Lunau/Photo Researchers, Inc.; 46tr: kluft/Wikipedia; 46l: Associated Press; 46rct: David Parker/Photo Researchers, Inc.; 46rcb: US Geological Survey; 46br: David Parker/Photo Researchers, Inc.; 47t, 47bl: Jeremy Bishop/Photo Researchers, Inc.; 47br: Stephen & Donna O'Meara/Photo Researchers, Inc.; 48r: Malcolm Teasdale; 49ct: US Navy photo by Photographer's Mate 2nd Class Philip A. McDaniel; 49cm: iStockphoto; 49cb: FabioConcetta/Dreamstime; 49bl: iStockphoto; 50tl: public domain; 50tr: iStockphoto; 50bl: arindambanerjee/Shutterstock; 50br: US Navy; 51tl: Logan Abassi/The United Nations Development Programme; 51cl: US Navy photo by Mass Communication Specialist 3rd Class Erin Olberholtzen; 51tr: Associated Press; 51bl: US Air Force; 51br: George Allen Penton/Shutterstock; 52l: punksid/Shutterstock; 52tc: Yuyang/Dreamstime; 52tr: Alfred Wegener Institute for Polar and Marine Research, Bremerhaven, Germany; 52bc: Alvinku/Shutterstock; 52–53: Romeo Ranoco/X00226/Reuters/Corbis; 54–55: Bruce Omori/epa/Corbis; 57 (ashes, lapilli, bomb): Gary Hincks/Photo Researchers, Inc.; 57 (ash particle): US Geological Survey; 57cr: Patrick Landmann/Photo Researchers, Inc.; 58–59: AFP/Getty Images; 58cl: Stephen & Donna O'Meara/Photo Researchers, Inc.; 58cm, 58bl, 58bc: public domain; 59c: OAR/National Undersea Research Program (NURP); 62–63: Gobierno de Álvaro Colom, Guatemala 2008–2012; 64l: Associated Press; 64c: public domain; 64r: Stringer Pakistan/Reuters; 66t, 66c: Associated Press; 66b: NASA; 66–67 (map): Jezper/Shutterstock; 67tl: PRILL Mediendesign und Fotografie/Shutterstock; 67tr, 67c, 67br: Associated Press; 68–69: Stringer Pakistan/Reuters; 70–71t: Associated Press; 70br: Gary Hincks/Photo Researchers, Inc.; 71bl: Associated Press; 71bc: Skynavin/Shutterstock; 71br: Imaginechina via AP Images; 72tc: public domain; 73tc: Georgette Douwma/Photo Researchers, Inc.; 73cr: NOAA/NGDC; 74tc: Fotograferad av Henryk Kotowski/Wikipedia; 74br: AFP/Getty Images; 75cr: US Navy photo by Photographer's Mate Airman Patrick M. Bonafede; 75cr: David Rydevik; 75bl, 75br: AFP/Getty Images; 76–77: Mainichi Newspaper/AFLO/Nippon News/Corbis; 78l: Tatiana Grozetskaya/Shutterstock; 78c: Lee Prince/Shutterstock; 78r: Eye of Science/Photo Researchers, Inc.; 80t: iStockphoto; 80c: Bettmann/Corbis; 80b: Janne Hämäläinen/Shutterstock; 80–81 (map): Jezper/Shutterstock; 81tl: gopixgo/Shutterstock; 81tr, 81c, 81bl: Associated Press; 81br: Sigit Pamungkas/Reuters; 82 (flame): Koteus/Shutterstock; 82 (leaf): shantiShanti/Shutterstock; 82 (fuel supply): Olexa/Shutterstock; 82 (weather): easyshoot/Shutterstock; 82 (type of land): iStockphoto; 82tr: Fletcher & Baylis/Photo Researchers, Inc.; 82–83: Associated Press; 83tl: Alexis Rosenfeld/Photo Researchers, Inc.; 83tr: Army Air Corps Photo 40400AC, copy provided by Dr. Robin Rose; 83bl: Photo Researchers, Inc.; 84–85: Stephen Morrison/epa/Corbis; 86 (background): Tatiana Grozetskaya/Shutterstock; 86 (factories icon): Dimec/Shutterstock; 86 (cattle icon): Amold11/Shutterstock; 86 (car exhaust icon): Arcady/Shutterstock; 86 (aerosols icon): Pelonmaker/Shutterstock; 87tr: Vitoriano Jr/Shutterstock; 87rc: Jezper/Shutterstock; 87 (laptop): iStockphoto; 88–89: Associated Press; 88bcl: Lee Prince/Shutterstock; 88bcr: Beth Swanson/Shutterstock; 88br: Doug Lemke/Shutterstock; 90tl: koya979/Shutterstock; 90cl: Tatonka/Shutterstock; 90cm: iStockphoto; 90br: EVB Energy Ltd/Wikipedia; 90bl (background): Ecocar Symbol/Shutterstock; 91cl: iStockphoto; 91cr: Drimi/Shutterstock; 91bl: pa3x/Shutterstock; 91bc: ively/Shutterstock; 91br: pa3x/Shutterstock; 92–93: NASA; 94tl: Fæ/Wikipedia; 94tc: Algoi/Shutterstock; 94tr: public domain; 94bc: Kirill Zdorov/Dreamstime; 94br, 95tl, 95tc, 95tr: public domain; 95br: Dr. Cecil H. Fox/Photo Researchers, Inc.; 96–97: Eye of Science/Photo Researchers, Inc.; 97rc: WHO 2012; 97br: Andy Crump, TDR, World Health Organization/Photo Researchers, Inc.; 98l: NASA; 98c: US Air Force photo by Senior Airman Joshua Strang; 98r, 100–101: David A. Hardy/AstroArt; 100lc: NASA; 101tr: Science Source/Photo Researchers, Inc.; 102tl, 102–103b: NASA; 103tl: Ensuper/Shutterstock; 103tr: US Air Force photo by Senior Airman Joshua Strang; 103br: iStockphoto; 104–105: NASA.

ARTWORK

20tr, 21tl, 24–25cb, 26–27t, 33bl, 33bc, 33br, 36cl, 36cm, 36cr, 44tr, 44b, 48lt, 48lc, 48lb, 56–57, 56l, 57cm, 57bc, 67bl, 72–73b, 91tr, 108: Tim Loughhead/Precision Illustration; all other artwork: Scholastic.

COVER

Front cover: UPI Photo/Landov. Back cover: (tr) Tim Loughhead/Precision Illustration; (computer monitor) Manaemedia/Dreamstime.

Key to symbols in **More here** columns

 Keywords for web searches

 *Suggested reading*

Watch on TV, on DVD, or online

View from far away

 Visit exciting places

Great things to do

 Mini-glossary

Credits and acknowledgments